LOZZY'S
COMPLETE GUIDE
TO
LENORMAND

WORKBOOK EDITION

LOZZY PHILLIPS

LOZZY'S COMPLETE GUIDE TO LENORMAND

Lozzy's Complete Guide To Lenormand
by Lozzy Phillips

Published by Lozzy's Lenormand

www.lozzyslenormand.com

© 2021 Lozzy Phillips

ISBN: 9781699277393

Contents

Introduction _____ 11

About This Book _____ 13

What is Lenormand? _____ 14

Quick Reference Lenormand Card Meanings _____ 22

I: Lenormand Card Meanings & Combinations:

About Lenormand Card Meanings _____ 27

The Importance of Card Combinations in Lenormand _____ 29

    1. Rider _____ 33

    2. Clover _____ 36

    3. Ship _____ 39

    4. House _____ 43

    5. Tree _____ 46

    6. Clouds _____ 49

    7. Snake _____ 51

    8. Coffin _____ 54

    9. Bouquet _____ 57

10. SCYTHE _____ 60

11. WHIP _____ 63

12. BIRDS _____ 66

13. CHILD _____ 69

14. FOX _____ 72

15. BEAR _____ 75

16. STARS _____ 78

17. STORKS _____ 81

18. DOG _____ 84

19. TOWER _____ 87

20. GARDEN _____ 90

21. MOUNTAIN _____ 93

22. CROSSROADS _____ 96

23. MICE _____ 99

24. HEART _____ 102

25. RING _____ 105

26. BOOK _____ 108

27. LETTER _____ 111

28. MAN _____ 114

29. WOMAN _____ 117

30. LILY _____ 120

31. SUN _____ 123

32. MOON _____ 126

33. KEY _____ 129

34. FISH _____ 132

35. ANCHOR _____ 135

36. CROSS _____ 138

II: LENORMAND CARD LAYOUTS:

CARD LAYOUT - BASICS _____ 142

STEP BY STEP GUIDE TO CARD LAYOUTS:

THE THREE-CARD SPREAD _____ 148

THE FIVE-CARD SPREAD _____ 152

THE NINE-CARD SPREAD _____ 157

THE GRAND TABLEAU _____ 163

    MIRRORING & REFLECTION _____ 165

    KNIGHTING _____ 167

HOUSES _____ 168

HOW TO READ THE GRAND TABLEAU _____ 171

III: LENORMAND IN PRACTICE

WORKING WITH LENORMAND CARDS IN PRACTICE _____ 186

    UNDERSTANDING CARD MEANINGS & CONTEXT _____ 187

    HOW TO GET MORE CONFIDENT WITH CARD MEANINGS _____ 190

        EXERCISE I: GETTING TO KNOW CARD MEANINGS _____ 194

        EXERCISE II: TEST YOURSELF ON CARD MEANINGS _____ 200

UNDERSTANDING CARD COMBINATIONS _____ 205

        EXERCISE III: MAKING CARD COMBINATIONS _____ 208

        EXERCISE IV: TEST YOURSELF ON CARD COMBINATIONS ____ 210

        EXERCISE V: CARD COMBINATIONS IN CONTEXT _____ 212

ABOUT LENORMAND QUESTIONS:

    POSITIVE & NEGATIVE MEANINGS: ANSWER YES OR NO? _____ 216

    ASKING LENORMAND QUESTIONS FOR THE BEST RESULTS _____ 219

    FUTURE, FATE & FREE WILL IN LENORMAND READINGS _____ 223

    TIPS FOR ASKING EMPOWERING LENORMAND QUESTIONS _____ 229

TELLING A STORY WITH LENORMAND _____ 236

Exercise VI: Telling Stories With Lenormand _____ 243

What About Lenormand Timings? _____ 248

Common Mistakes When Reading Lenormand Cards For Yourself 256

Keeping A Lenormand Journal _____ 260

Building Up To Reading For Other People _____ 264

A Note About Choosing Lenormand Decks _____ 270

Practice Readings _____ 275

Answers _____ 287

INTRODUCTION

I've long been a fan of fortune-telling cards.

My journey into cartomancy began many years ago using Tarot, but in recent years I found myself drawn to the more upfront, storytelling nature of the Lenormand, which doesn't have the mythic, subjective associations of the Tarot. With the Lenormand, what you see is what you get; the symbols are simple, universal and related to people's day-to-day lives. As more of an earthy and nature-loving than an esoteric person, this became a more appealing approach for me. With Lenormand, it's the particular card combinations that give the story of the reading – as well as the context in which the cards are read.

Like Tarot, Lenormand cards all have symbols; unlike the Tarot system, however, each card does not represent a particular stage on a journey, and there are no major and minor arcana. Lenormand symbols are very direct; a Key for the 'answer', for example, or a Book to represent 'knowledge'; a Ship is a journey of some kind, a Snake is a betrayal or problem. The Rider represents an arrival; the Sun, success.

There are various Lenormand decks; the traditional eighteenth century decks, usually with playing-card inserts, and countless more modern versions, many of which are beautiful and would be a positive addition to anybody's collection. The beauty of Lenormand, however, is that because the **symbols** are universal, it is possible for anybody to make their own versions of the cards, which will have the added advantage of having a more personalised feel for them. In this book, I'm focusing on the images I use on my website, rather than on one deck or another, but I have some tips on choosing a deck at the end of the book. There are many individual artists making their own versions also, and again, many of these are beautiful, so do consider supporting an artist if you're looking for a deck with something a bit different.

I've found the accuracy of readings with Lenormand cards to be quite startling at times, and thus have found them useful for guidance and support in all sorts of situations. I read the cards for myself and for others and I love experimenting with them. I've put this book together to help share all I've learned, and some techniques you can use to make the most of the cards yourself.

Happy reading!

Lozzy x

ABOUT THIS BOOK

The book is designed to be a *practical* guide to starting to read the Lenormand cards and beginning to develop a regular Lenormand practice. It includes both information and guidance, as well as practical exercises and tasks, to help deepen your understanding. Part I is mainly for reference. Part II takes you into more depth, addressing common questions and problems, and giving you practical tasks and exercises to help test and deepen your understanding of the cards and develop your own practice.

The **Card Meanings and Combinations** section begins with a handy overview of all the main card meanings in different contexts & their messages, followed by card combination lists for all 36 Lenormand Cards. It is intended as a **quick guide** for looking up meanings, and double-checking your understanding of the cards.

The **Lenormand Card Layouts** section takes you step by step through the main Lenormand layouts, with detailed examples.

The **Lenormand In Practice** section then goes into more depth about reading Lenormand in practice, getting confident with and applying card meanings in more depth in different contexts such as Love & Relationships and Career, as well as addressing many of the issues and questions that new Lenormand practitioners come up against in their regular practice.

Throughout the book & at the end you will find **Exercises, & Practice Readings** to help you cement your understanding of the Lenormand system.

What Is Lenormand?

Lenormand is a cartomancy system, ostensibly based on the methods used by famed French fortune-teller Mademoiselle Marie Lenormand but in truth, renamed in 18th century Germany after her death to capitalise both on her name and on the fashion for fortune-telling parlour games. Mlle Lenormand herself achieved fame and notoriety in Paris during the Napoleonic era and beyond, and was said to have advised Napoleon himself and his lover Josephine, as well as leading French Revolutionary figures such as Robespierre and Marat. However, as far as we know, she never shared her methods. A 56 card fortune-telling method *The Grand Jeu de Lenormand* was published in France several years after her death. This bears little relation to what we know as Lenormand today. The current Lenormand system, otherwise known as *Le Petit Jeu*, is instead based on a deck devised by one Johann Kaspar Hechtel, a German factory owner, in around 1799, as a parlour game he called "The Game of Hope" (*Das Spiel Der Hoffnung*). It is this deck that was renamed and re-marketed after Mlle Lenormand's death, and these cards we generally refer to when talking about Lenormand as it is today.

A standard Petit Lenormand deck consists of 36 cards, including the two which represent the possible Querents, The Woman and The Man. The other 34 cards are depictions of either day to day objects and places—Key, Book, House—or of animals (Bear, Fox, Snake), and each has an associated playing card equivalent. Each Lenormand symbol has an underlying meaning, which represents a universal or fundamental facet of day to day life. The meanings of different cards are combined to create new meanings, and there a number of specific layouts which work well with the Lenormand system in order to deepen meaning and understanding and form a complete narrative.

As such, Lenormand is really a storytelling system. It works like a language, with each card like a word, that combines meaningfully with other cards in a given context into sentences, paragraphs and whole stories. The simplicity and directness of the symbols makes it relatively easy to learn, while the combinations in context add depth and understanding and add up to a complete picture, if you will, of a given situation.

From a practical viewpoint, you'll need the following to really understand the Lenormand system and get it working for you:

✢ The underlying meanings of all 36 Lenormand cards
✢ The ability to apply those meanings in different day to day contexts
✢ An understanding of the ways the cards combine to form new meanings
✢ The main Lenormand layouts and their uses
✢ The ability to pull together the layouts, context and card combinations into coherent stories, in order to answer specific questions.

How Lenormand Differs From Tarot

As many would-be readers come to Lenormand, as I did a long time ago, from Tarot, it's worth taking a look at some of the main differences between the two card-reading systems. It's not just that these are two sets of cards with different symbols, and it's not the case that you can just use them interchangeably, in layouts, say, as the two systems work in very different ways, with a different ethos and approach.

If you truly want to get the most from what the Lenormand system has to offer, there are some key adjustments I'd advise you to make in your approach if you're coming to it from Tarot.

So what are the main things to be aware of?

There are only 36 cards, and they all carry equal "weight"

Tarot, of course, has its 78 cards; its four suits, the Minor Arcana, all depicting the various stages of progress on the 'journey' of that suit, as well as the Major Arcana, the big symbols of life. Tarot – at least, as it is used today—symbolically has a strong sense of the spiritual journey about it, of a working to a higher level, of uncovering the mysteries of the universe, being "allowed in" to discover great secrets, of spiritual discovery and a higher power.

Lenormand Symbols

There is no such division in the Lenormand Cards. Each of the 36 cards has **one** symbol, no one symbol is deemed "higher" in the sense of being more important or further along a spiritual path than another, and the **underlying meaning** of each symbol remains the same regardless of a deck's imagery. (More on that issue later). All Lenormand symbols relate to everyday things, objects and concerns, the day-to-day of ordinary people's lives. That doesn't make such concerns "lesser" or "base" though, although I have sometimes seen the Lenormand system characterised that way, for example, with Tarot as supposedly "more psychological and deeper," and Lenormand deemed more "ordinary and everyday."

While there is some truth behind that division, I don't think day to day concerns are "lesser," in any way. As humans, we all know what love feels like, value friendships and homes and family, understand the need for safety and having enough resources to live day to day. There's our **Heart, Dog, House** cards. We make commitments and promises **(Ring)** we deal with officials or status issues **(Tower)** we go from childhood to adulthood to old age (**Child, Lily**), we learn things, face challenges, make changes in our lives, deal with problems, sadness, happiness, the lot. They are **universal.** And universality is one of the keys to the Lenormand system.

Lenormand is more direct, grounded and blunt than Tarot

That said, Lenormand is less of an esoteric, mystical system. It does, like all cartomancy systems, involve a degree of unlocking mysteries and truths but there is far less of the 'initiation' element, of the 'being party to a higher power', to spiritual awakening. It is more about uncovering what is there, seeing what is already in front of your eyes. Grounded, and fairly earth-bound.

If I had to personify the Tarot, I would picture a teacher, a guide, a higher power, with an air of mystery, giving me the keys to many-layered secrets. Lenormand? More that tactless but spot-on relative or neighbour who will tell you exactly what they think of your life whether you asked their opinion or not!

Lenormand meanings work from the inside out, not the outside in

From my own experience, I've found interpreting Lenormand basically works from the core outwards. To read and understand Lenormand, you take the **most fundamental**, **universal meaning** of that card and its symbol and you apply it outwards to the context and world you are in. You then combine it with the meanings of surrounding cards, also in that context to give nuance. The individual card meaning itself is like a seed, which can then grow and branches out to meet the world in which it resides.

Tarot, however, is rather more exploratory. It deals with more spiritual, so-called "higher" concepts, and has a more intellectual, or some might even say, elitist, element (if you know a little of the history of Tarot, you will see how that side of it came about.) The nuance is in the symbolism itself and the ins and outs of that. To access the knowledge the Tarot brings, you as a reader come to it from the outside in. It is the cards themselves that give you a doorway in a way. It's why meditating on a Tarot card, for instance, is pretty effective; most of the nuance already contained in the card and you dive deeper and deeper into that and explore it further, discovering more and more in the process.

Lenormand does not use card reversals

Tarot cards have a whole extra generated set of meanings when the card is reversed; usually the negative aspects of each card's meanings. This isn't the case for Lenormand, although there is a method of traditional Lenormand reading called the Near and Far method which does something similar, depending on whether the card is near or far from the Querent in the layout. It is mainly for use in the Grand Tableau, and as I, like many readers, don't generally use it, I am not including Near and Far meanings in this book.

Instead, there are specific cards in a Lenormand deck which generally have either positive or negative meanings. These will be covered later in the book, in the section on Yes/No Answers. Secondly, the negativity or positivity of a card is deeply affected by the *surrounding* cards, as well as card order.

This is because the Lenormand system is based primarily on card combinations, rather than single cards. The fullest meaning of Lenormand cards comes not through the meanings of individual cards but from *combining* each one with others to tell a story. That is where you get the full picture of Lenormand; that is where all the nuance, detail and story generation lies.

As with a word in a language, each Lenormand card is like a building block with regard to the bigger picture. It's not true that you cannot consider each card by itself; after all, such universal life concepts as "Love" "Fate" "Family" "Safety" are hardly meaningless ideas. However, you will get much more from the Lenormand system from combining the cards to create and generate new meanings. It makes the system creative, expansive and outward-looking. It puts fundamental concepts and things and people and situations together to generate new meanings; hundreds and hundreds of them are possible from the seed of just one card.

Lenormand is more of a conceptual (& practical) than a visual system

Lenormand is often compared to a spoken or written language, and with good reason. It works in much the same way. Language starts with a core, universal, fundamental concept that you then create a word for. The word is simply a symbol of that concept. Your 'word' could be in any language, be made up of those in the English alphabet, or in Cyrillic script, or in Chinese symbols. It could be made up of Egyptian-style hieroglyphics. It could, as in most Lenormand decks, be made up of a drawing or illustration that represents, usually fairly simply, that concept or thing. That symbol is just your means of communicating that concept. But however you do it, it **still represents the same basic underlying idea.**

And just as with language,,in Lenormand, those concepts combine, into sentences and paragraphs to tell a story. Often that combination changes, gives nuance to or magnifies those meanings. A whole new "meaning" is created; in a sentence, a paragraph, ten paragraphs, a whole book. The situation you're using them in also impacts that. Only with all elements present do you have the big picture.

But Tarot doesn't work this way. It is about spiritual discovery. You discover the concept *through* the imagery in the individual cards and relate them to where they are placed in a given spread. It's like a gateway. Yes, there are "concepts" behind the symbols, but they are spiritual in nature. You use the cards themselves to explore the concepts. Your cards are a tool for that discovery and all its nuances. The symbols in the Tarot cards themselves matter hugely in this.

Lenormand meaning stays the same regardless of card design

As well as the idea of working from the inside out rather than the outside in, this is an absolutely crucial difference between how the Lenormand and Tarot systems work at their best. Underlying concept, not representation or manifestation, is more important, so do bear that in mind when you are choosing your decks.

Artwork is irrelevant to Lenormand meanings

This can throw some readers who are more used to Tarot and are used to exploring the hidden meanings and symbols in the visual image, or the cards to deepen meaning. Think of all the symbols that are hidden in the classic Rider-Waite deck, for instance, all of which add depth to our understanding of the card. Not so in Lenormand.

But it doesn't matter one bit in terms of card meaning whether your Lenormand card is a word written on a playing card, a computer graphic, a photo you took on your phone, an elaborate gothic design, an 18th century illustration, an exquisitely hand-painted watercolour, an Art Deco scene. It doesn't matter if your House has a path, trees and big garden, or just a cottage on its own or is a kids' drawing. It's still a House and most fundamentally means "Home" – the rest of the design is wholly irrelevant to the meaning. Any versions are manifestations of that same basic concept.

Sure, you may have a personal *preference* in terms of design, you may want your cards to reflect your sensibilities and use them to draw you better into the single fundamental meaning of that particular card. I do too, and I love checking out different decks and picking those that appeal to me aesthetically. But that really is all it is: personal preference. Just bear in mind that although the imagery we prefer can help us resonate with the cards, beautiful, design, artwork and exploration of imagery is not at heart what the Lenormand system is about.

So in summary, then, some of the biggest differences between Lenormand and Tarot:

- ♣ Le Petit Lenormand has 36 cards, the Tarot 78, split into Major & Minor Arcana
- ♣ Lenormand is much more direct, often to the point of bluntness! It is less of an exploratory or 'spiritual' system, and speaks more to everyday concerns. That doesn't make it less 'meaningful'.

✤ Lenormand works from the inside out, based on universal core meanings

✤ In Tarot, meaning comes mainly through individual cards. In Lenormand most of the meaning, detail and nuance comes from combining the cards.

✤ You don't have reversed cards in Lenormand, but in Tarot, all cards have a reversed meaning

✤ Lenormand works more like a language, with a basic underlying meaning behind the card.

✤ The artwork and design can add nuance to the meaning in Tarot. This is not the case in Lenormand, where a card's meaning is always exactly the same across designs

Quick Reference
Lenormand Card Meanings

1. Rider   Arrival, New Situation or Individual, News; Upcoming

2. Clover   Luck, Opportunities, Chance

3. Ship   Journey, Travel, Transport, Movement

4. House   House, Home, Family, Family Name

5. Tree   Health, Healing, Spirituality, Growth

6. Clouds   Confusion, Uncertainty, Lack of Clarity

7. Snake   Betrayal, Big Problems, Untrustworthiness

8. Coffin   The End, Death, Ending, Finality

9. Bouquet   Loveliness, Beauty, Blessings, Gifts

10. Scythe   Cut, Decision, Reduction, Sudden, Hurt

11. Whip   A Hard Time, Abuse, Hard Work, Physical Activity, Sex

12. Birds   Conversation, Talk, Chatter, Discussion

13. Child   Child, Youngster, Beginner

14. Fox   Work, Survival, Cunning, Theft

15. Bear   Money, Finances, Wealth, Power, Weight

16. Stars   Fame, Achievement, Goals, Famous or Admired Person

17. Storks   Fresh start, New Beginnings, Starting Again

18. Dog   Friendship, Friends, Allies, Soulmates, Loyalty

19. Tower   Buildings, Corporations, Officialdom, Status, Height

20. GARDEN	NETWORK, MARKETPLACE, GROUP, SOCIAL LIFE, PUBLIC, EVENT
21. MOUNTAIN	BLOCK, RIGIDITY, DELAY, OBSTACLE
22. CROSSROADS	OPTIONS, CHOICES, MULTIPLES, FORK IN THE ROAD
23. MICE	WORRIES, ANXIETY, TROUBLES, STRESS
24. HEART	LOVE, PASSION, LOVE-LIFE, CARING, CORE
25. RING	RELATIONSHIP, CONTRACT, PAYMENT, MARRIAGE, BOND
26. BOOK	KNOWLEDGE, LEARNING, SECRETS, STUDY
27. LETTER	LETTER, NEWS, MESSAGE, WRITTEN DOCUMENT
28. MAN	MAN, THE QUESTIONER, MALE, MASCULINE
29. WOMAN	WOMAN, THE QUESTIONER, FEMALE, FEMININE
30. LILY	AGE, OLDER PERSON, RETIREMENT, LATER LIFE, MATURITY
31. SUN	SUCCESS, HAPPINESS, JOY, SUNSHINE
32. MOON	EMOTIONS, CREATIVITY, FEELINGS
33. KEY	DESTINY, FATE, SIGNIFICANCE, IMPORTANCE, KARMA
34. FISH	BUSINESS, FREELANCING, INDEPENDENCE, CASHFLOW
35. ANCHOR	STABILITY, THE LONG TERM, PERMANENCE
36. CROSS	BURDEN, WORRIES, DEPRESSION, RELIGION, NEGATIVITY

I

LENORMAND CARD

MEANINGS

& COMBINATIONS

About Lenormand Card Meanings

Understanding—*really* understanding— the underlying Lenormand card meanings is the key to working with the cards and getting them to work for you. So in this section, I'm giving you detailed meanings & "messages" for each of the 36 cards in different contexts as well as the card combinations for that card. I should point out, though, that I'm providing these lists primarily for ease of reference and as a quick guide and overview rather than for you to try and learn by rote. Reference lists like these can be especially helpful when you are first learning the system and practising Lenormand card layouts.

As mentioned in the introduction, the particular deck you use should NOT affect the meanings. The symbols of each card should mean the same things across all decks, regardless of any imagery or design features in that particular deck, and you could just as easily use the playing card equivalent (although it's meaningless without some reference to the symbol) or just the word on a card. You *will* find there are some minor differences in how individual readers interpret the symbols, however. This can overcomplicate matters, especially for beginners.

One thing I'd suggest as you begin your Lenormand journey is to start making it a habit to consider different aspects of those real-life symbols for yourself. The Lenormand cards have a long history partly because the symbols used are universal, and speak to universal human concerns. As you begin to familiarise yourself with the cards, try to think about the following:

- ✤ What does that object, or thing make me think of in real life?
- ✤ If it's an animal, what are the commonly known features of that animal?
- ✤ What aspects of our culture does each object, thing or animal bring to mind?

✤ What cultural and historical meanings and differences might there be in the meaning of that symbol?

In Part III of this book, we will be looking at how you can deepen your understanding of the symbols further, and build your confidence in reading them independently.

THE IMPORTANCE OF CARD COMBINATIONS IN LENORMAND

Nearly all Lenormand card readings and layouts rely on the reader being able to interpret the cards in pairs, or combinations. If you know how to combine two cards with different meanings into one meaning, and understand how that works, then you will be able to read *any* Lenormand spread. This is why Lenormand Card Combination lists on websites and in books have proved so popular: they provide a quick point of reference, especially for beginners.

A word of warning, though. No card combination list is ever going to give you every single possible interpretation of every single combination. Even if you just came up with **one** meaning for each possible pair of cards in order, that would be **1296** possible meanings. And that, as I say, is a minimum. Most card combination lists will include two or three possible meanings for each. So... well. You do the math.

Instead, as you progress with Lenormand, you will find that the meanings given on the lists generally consist of just **the most common** interpretations. Don't get me wrong: card combination lists are an extremely useful reference to lean on, especially when you are just starting out, or when you're unsure, just need a quick reference and would like to feel a bit more confident in your readings. But if you want to become a more intuitive and accurate reader, you will at some point need to move beyond the lists, and start interpreting cards and card combinations by yourself.

LENORMAND CARD COMBINATIONS: THE #1 SECRET

When I was first learning Lenormand, the hardest thing to remember was the card combinations. I used to go back to my books again and again, and spend time searching for lists and interpretations, desperately trying to memorise them all. I know from the Lozzy's Lenormand blog that it is the card combination lists that my readers often head for first of all. But wouldn't you like to know *how* readers like me come up with those interpretations?

To understand how card combinations work, you need two things. The first is, as we said above, an understanding of each individual card meaning. The second is the knowledge of **how the cards work together in pairs**. Lenormand is a storytelling system, and it works by linking pairs of cards together into a narrative. So here is a quick trick for understanding how they do that.

- ♣ The **first** card in the pair can be read as a **Noun** - a thing, a person, a name
- ♣ The **second** card in a pair can be read as an **Adjective** - the *description or modifier* of that thing or person

Examples:

SUN + MOUNTAIN: Success (Noun) + Blocked/Delayed (Adjective)
Meaning: Blocked/Delayed Success

MAN + BOUQUET: Man (Noun) + Pleasant/Good-looking (Adjective)
Meaning: Pleasant or Good-looking Man

When you read through the combination lists that follow, bear this method in mind to see how I've come up with the meanings I have. Sometimes you'll find you do have to use a bit of intuition, your knowledge of the world, and some lateral thinking to find a realistic meaning for a particular combination.

As you deepen your understanding of the Lenormand cards and their meanings, you will begin to appreciate how any given pair of cards could in practice have a multitude of meanings. It's for this reason that no card combination list can be considered to be definitive, That said, they are highly useful as reference when you are starting to learn the cards.

In **Part III** of this book, we will be making further use of this knowledge and giving you plenty of practice of coming up with card combination interpretations for yourself.

Let's start first with looking at the cards in a bit more depth. Although the cards and methods I use are image-only, as many Lenormand decks include playing card references, I've included the relevant playing card reference in the descriptions. For each card, I'm giving you both nouns and adjectives, the likely meanings in several reading contexts, and the basic "message" from each card.

I. RIDER

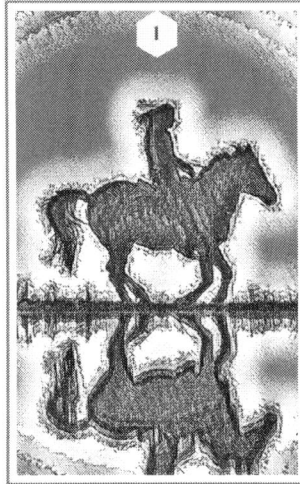

Playing Card	**Nine of Hearts**
General (Noun)	Arrival, Visit, Visitor, Delivery, News, Something New
General (Adj)	Upcoming, On The Way, Approaching, New
Love	New Lover, New Romantic Situation, Upcoming Romance
Career	Offer, New Job Role On The Way, Upcoming Change, Delivery
People	Outgoing, Energetic, Up For New Things
Timing	Soon, Next, A Day, Week, Month, First of the Month, January

Card's Message

Something or someone is coming into your life - and soon! What can you see coming over the horizon? What's updating in your life? Are you ready and open to receive it?

RIDER CARD COMBINATIONS

RIDER & CLOVER	CHANCE ARRIVAL OR ENCOUNTER; LUCK ON THE WAY
RIDER & SHIP	OVERSEAS VISITOR OR NEWS, FLEETING ENCOUNTER, DELIVERY
RIDER & HOUSE	HOUSE OR FAMILY NEWS; HOUSE GUEST; VISITOR; NEW HOUSE
RIDER & TREE	SPIRITUAL ENCOUNTER, IMPROVED HEALTH UPCOMING
RIDER & CLOUDS	CONFUSING NEWS OR MESSAGE; UPCOMING UNCERTAINTY
RIDER & SNAKE	DIFFICULT NEWS; ONCOMING CHALLENGES; PROBLEMS AHEAD
RIDER & COFFIN	BIG CHANGES, PERIOD OF TRANSITION, MOURNING; FINAL VISIT
RIDER & BOUQUET	GOOD THINGS AHEAD, HAPPY NEWS, GIFT DELIVERY
RIDER & SCYTHE	SEPARATION, SUDDEN DECISION, ACCIDENT NEWS
RIDER & WHIP	SEXUAL ENCOUNTER; ARGUMENT; HARD TIMES COMING
RIDER & BIRDS	ANNOUNCEMENTS; NEWS; PHONE CALLS
RIDER & CHILD	PREGNANCY NEWS; BIRTH ANNOUNCEMENTS
RIDER & FOX	JOB NEWS; NEW EMPLOYEE
RIDER & BEAR	MONEY ARRIVING; FINANCIAL NEWS
RIDER & STARS	ACHIEVEMENT NEWS; HOPE; ASSISTANCE
RIDER & STORKS	FRESH START COMING; CHANGES AHEAD
RIDER & DOG	FRIEND'S NEWS; FRIEND VISITING
RIDER & TOWER	BUSINESS ACQUISITION; OFFICIAL STATUS COMING

RIDER & GARDEN	NETWORKING; UPCOMING SOCIALIZING; GUESTS
RIDER & MOUNTAIN	DELAYS AHEAD; SLOWING DOWN
RIDER & CROSSROAD	CHOICES AHEAD; NEW POSSIBILITIES
RIDER & MICE	WORRYING NEWS; STRESSFUL TIMES
RIDER & HEART	NEW LOVER; GREATER INTIMACY
RIDER & RING	COMMITMENT; PROPOSAL; NEW CONTRACT; MARRIAGE
RIDER & BOOK	DISCOVERY; LESSON; NEW PROJECT
RIDER & LETTER	NEWS; MESSAGE; MAIL; DOCUMENTS; DELIVERY
RIDER & MAN	NEW MAN IN YOUR LIFE; MAN'S NEWS; MALE VISITOR
RIDER & WOMAN	NEW WOMAN IN YOUR LIFE; WOMAN'S NEWS; FEMALE VISITOR
RIDER & LILY	AGEING; ARRIVAL OF WISDOM; PENDING RETIREMENT
RIDER & SUN	SUCCESS IS COMING; VICTORY; ACHIEVEMENT
RIDER & MOON	NEW ROMANCE; UPCOMING CREATIVE PERIOD; RUSH OF EMOTIONS
RIDER & KEY	SIGNIFICANT EVENT COMING; SPIRITUAL LESSON; TURNING POINT
RIDER & FISH	NEW BUSINESS; INDEPENDENCE COMING
RIDER & ANCHOR	ABOUT TO SETTLE DOWN; STABILITY COMING; REASSURANCE
RIDER & CROSS	PAINFUL TIMES; CONCERNS AHEAD; A LIFE TEST COMING

2. CLOVER

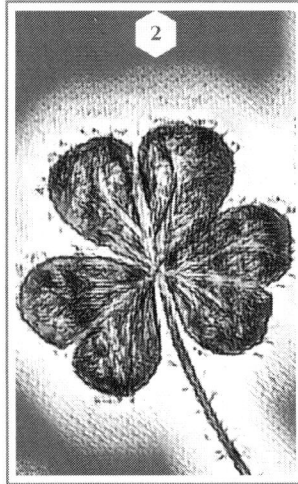

Playing Card:	**Six of Diamonds**
General (Noun)	Luck, Good Fortune, Opportunity, Gamble, Chance
General (Adj)	Fortunate, Lucky, Random, Opportunistic
Love:	Happiness, Lucky Opportunity, Chance Meeting
Career:	Lucky Turn, Win, Surprise Luck, Sudden Opportunity
People:	Risk-Taker, Gambler, Opportunist, Chancer, Spontaneous
Timing:	February, Two Weeks, Days, Months, Second of the Month

Card's Message

Fortune favours the brave! Take your chances; luck is on your side. Be open to random opportunities - you never know when or where they'll arise!

Clover Card Combinations

Clover & Rider	UPCOMING OPPORTUNITY; LUCK OR A WIN ON THE WAY
Clover & Ship	OVERSEAS OPPORTUNITY; LAST-MINUTE TRAVEL; HAPPY TRIP
Clover & House	PROSPEROUS FAMILY; HAPPY HOME
Clover & Tree	RECOVERY; GREAT HEALTH; SPIRITUAL PROTECTION
Clover & Clouds.	DODGY OPPORTUNITIES; GAMBLING ADDICTION; FOOLISHNESS
Clover & Snake	OPPORTUNIST; GAMBLER; FALSE OPPORTUNITY
Clover & Coffin.	RISKY SITUATION; MISFORTUNE; LUCK ENDS; UNLUCKY OUTCOME
Clover & Bouquet	GOOD LUCK; HAPPINESS; LOVELY SURPRISE;
Clover & Scythe	STROKE OF LUCK; SUDDEN OPPORTUNITY
Clover & Whip	HARD WORK BRINGS LUCK; HARD-WON VICTORY;
Clover & Birds	LUCKY CONVERSATIONS; LUCKY PARTNERSHIPS
Clover & Child	BEGINNER'S LUCK; SURPRISE PREGNANCY; HAPPY CHILD
Clover & Fox	JOB OR CAREER OPPORTUNITY; PROMOTION; LUCK AT WORK
Clover & Bear	UNEXPECTED WINDFALL; WIN; FINANCIAL OPPORTUNITY
Clover & Stars	VERY GOOD LUCK; SURPRISE FAME; LUCKY CHANCES
Clover & Storks	POSITIVE CHANGE; NEW START IMPROVES THINGS
Clover & Dog	FRIEND'S LUCK; POSITIVE INFLUENCES; GOOD FRIENDSHIPS
Clover & Tower	STATUS LUCK; CASINOS; HIGH STATUS OPPORTUNITIES

CLOVER & GARDEN	LOTTERY; GAMES; PUBLIC OPPORTUNITY
CLOVER & MOUNTAIN	RETREAT; HOLIDAY; BLOCKED OPPORTUNITIES
CLOVER & CROSSROAD	MULTIPLE OPPORTUNITIES; BREAKTHROUGH;
CLOVER & MICE	NERVOUS ANTICIPATION, BUTTERFLIES; GAMBLING WORRIES
CLOVER & HEART	LOVE OPPORTUNITY; IN LOVE; LUCKY LOVE RELATIONSHIP
CLOVER & RING	LUCKY ASSOCIATION OR CONTRACT; HAPPY MARRIAGE
CLOVER & BOOK	REVELATIONS, DISCOVERIES; LEARNING OPPORTUNITY
CLOVER & LETTER	LUCKY NEWS; WIN OR OFFER NOTIFICATION; LOTTERY TICKET
CLOVER & MAN	LUCKY MAN; OPPORTUNIST; POSITIVE THINKER; RISK TAKER
CLOVER & WOMAN	LUCKY WOMAN; OPPORTUNIST; RISK TAKER
CLOVER & LILY	LUCK BORNE OUT OF EXPERIENCE; HAPPY RETIREMENT
CLOVER & SUN	OVERNIGHT SUCCESS; AMAZING ACHIEVEMENT
CLOVER & MOON	CREATIVE OR ROMANTIC OPPORTUNITIES; ROMANTIC LUCK
CLOVER & KEY	LUCKY BREAK; POSITIVE TWIST OF FATE;
CLOVER & FISH	BUSINESS OPPORTUNITY; PROSPERITY, FINANCIAL LUCK
CLOVER & ANCHOR	LONG-TERM PROSPERITY; ALWAYS FALLING ON FEET
CLOVER & CROSS	THINGS WORK OUT IN THE END; SILVER LINING

3. SHIP

Playing Card:	**Ten of Spades**
General (Noun)	Travel, Journey, Trip, Overseas, Transport, Transfer, Movement
General (Adj)	Moving, Mobile, Travelling, Foreign, Overseas, Distant
Love:	Holiday Romance, Overseas Love, Long-Distance Affair
Career:	Global, Travel-Related, Jet-Setting, International
People:	Travellers, Foreigners, Vacationers, Naval Officers
Timing:	March, Three Weeks, Days, Months, Third of the Month

Card's Message

There's a whole world out there to explore. Where are you going? Is it time for an adventure; for new cultural influences, a change of scene? Shake things up a bit; don't stay put, get moving.

SHIP CARD COMBINATIONS

SHIP & RIDER   RETURN; ROUND TRIP; UPCOMING JOURNEY

SHIP & CLOVER   LUCKY JOURNEY; ENTERTAINING TRIP

SHIP & HOUSE   HOUSEBOAT; IMMIGRATION/EMIGRATION; MOVING AWAY

SHIP & TREE   SPIRITUAL JOURNEY; HEALTH-RELATED TRIP; SPA HOLIDAY

SHIP & CLOUDS   TRANSIENCE; ADVENTURE; UNCERTAIN JOURNEY

SHIP & SNAKE   DIFFICULT TRIP; BUMPY RIDE; TRAVEL PROBLEMS

SHIP & COFFIN   JOURNEY'S END; CANCELLED TRIP; FINAL JOURNEY

SHIP & BOUQUET   PLEASANT TRIP; LUXURY TRAVEL; CRUISE

SHIP & SCYTHE   TRIP CUT SHORT; LAST-MINUTE CANCELLATION; ACCIDENT

SHIP & WHIP   ROUGH JOURNEY; SPORTS TRIP; SEXUAL JOURNEY

SHIP & BIRDS   FOREIGN LANGUAGE; PLANE; PASSENGERS; TOURISTS

SHIP & CHILD   PREGNANCY KID'S TRIP; BEGINNER'S JOURNEY

SHIP & FOX   WORK TRAVEL; TRAVEL EMPLOYEE; STOWAWAY

SHIP & BEAR   MONEY TRANSFER; OVERSEAS MONEY; POWER HANDOVER

SHIP & STARS   SPACE EXPLORATION, ROCKET; FLYING; JOURNEY TO FAME

SHIP & STORKS   MOVING ON; START OF A NEW JOURNEY

SHIP & DOG   INTERNATIONAL FRIENDS; TRAVEL COMPANION

SHIP & TOWER   OFFICIAL TRIP; FOREIGN COMPANY OR GOVERNMENT

SHIP & GARDEN	GROUP TRIP; WORLD TRAVEL; FOREIGN COUNTRIES
SHIP & MOUNTAIN	DELAYED TRIP; BLOCKED JOURNEY; BORDERS
SHIP & CROSSROAD	MULTIPLE TRIPS; CHOICE OF ROUTE; EXCURSIONS
SHIP & MICE	STRESSFUL TRIP; ANXIOUS JOURNEY
SHIP & HEART	ROMANTIC TRIP; HOLIDAY ROMANCE; OVERSEAS LOVE
SHIP & RING	HONEYMOON; OVERSEAS WEDDING; FOREIGN CONTRACT
SHIP & BOOK	RESEARCH; JOURNEY TO PUBLICATION; EDUCATIONAL TRIP
SHIP & LETTER	TRAVEL DOCUMENTS; OVERSEAS NEWS; LETTER IN TRANSIT
SHIP & MAN	MALE TRAVELER; FOREIGNER
SHIP & WOMAN.	FEMALE TRAVELER; FOREIGNER
SHIP & LILY	EXTENDED TRIP; OLDER TRAVELLER
SHIP & SUN	SUCCESSFUL JOURNEY; HOT COUNTRY; SUMMER HOLIDAY
SHIP & MOON	DAY-DREAMS; CREATIVE JOURNEY; OVERNIGHT TRAVEL; MOOD SWINGS
SHIP & KEY	SIGNIFICANT JOURNEY; KARMA; TRIP OF A LIFETIME
SHIP & FISH	BUSINESS TRIP; TRANSPORTATION; TRADE
SHIP & ANCHOR	NEVER-ENDING JOURNEY; LONG TRIP; ARRIVAL
SHIP & CROSS	PILGRIMAGE, RELIGIOUS JOURNEY; PROBLEMATIC TRIP

4. HOUSE

Playing Card:	**King of Hearts**
General (Noun):	House, Home, Family, Family Name, Real Estate
General (Adj):	Domestic, Intimate, Warm, Loving
Love:	Hearth & Home, Loved Ones, Family Life, Core, Warmth
Career:	Home-Working, Domestic Business, Family Business
People:	Traditional, Homebody, Domesticated, Family-Oriented
Timing:	April, Four Days, Weeks, Months

Card's Message

Home is where the heart is. Who is the real you when nobody is looking, when there is nobody to impress? Hunker down under the duvet or spend time reconnecting with your family and loved ones.

House Card Combinations

HOUSE & RIDER	VISIT; GUEST; GUESTHOUSE
HOUSE & CLOVER	FORTUNATE FAMILY; GOOD LOCATION; NICE PLACE
HOUSE & SHIP	MOVING HOUSE; MOVING AWAY; HOUSEBOAT; CAMPER VAN
HOUSE & TREE	HEALTH CENTRE; SPIRITUAL HOME; KARMIC FAMILY
HOUSE & CLOUDS	DOMESTIC ISSUES; PROBLEMS AT HOME;
HOUSE & SNAKE	ABUSIVE HOME OR FAMILY; DOMESTIC ARGUMENTS
HOUSE & COFFIN	FAMILY DEATH; HOUSE SALE
HOUSE & BOUQUET	LOVELY HOME; INTERIOR DESIGN; PLEASANT FAMILY
HOUSE & SCYTHE	SEPARATION, FAMILY SPLIT; SUDDEN HOUSE SALE
HOUSE & WHIP	DOMESTIC QUARRELS; GYM; BORDELLO
HOUSE & BIRDS	DOMESTIC PARTNERS; HOUSEMATES; MEETING-HOUSE
HOUSE & CHILD	CHILDHOOD HOME; STARTER HOME; SMALL HOUSE
HOUSE & FOX	BUILDER; HOMEWORKER; DOMESTIC EMPLOYEE; AGENCY
HOUSE & BEAR	BUY-TO-LET; WEALTHY OR POWERFUL FAMILY
HOUSE & STARS	DREAM HOUSE; CELEBRITY HOME; FAMOUS FAMILY
HOUSE & STORKS	NEW HOME; MOVING HOUSE; HOUSE EXTENSION
HOUSE & DOG	PETS; FRIENDLY FAMILY; FRIEND'S HOUSE; HOUSEMATES
HOUSE & TOWER	FLATS, TOWER BLOCK; HOUSING ASSOC; ESTATE AGENCY

HOUSE & GARDEN	BIG FAMILY; STATELY HOME; PUB, CAFE; THEATRE
HOUSE & MOUNTAIN	BLOCKED HOUSE-SALE; CHALET; REMOTE LOCATION
HOUSE & CROSSROAD	MULTIPLE HOMES; CHOICE OF HOUSES
HOUSE & MICE	DOMESTIC WORRIES; ANXIOUS MOVE; WORRIED FAMILY
HOUSE & HEART	LOVING HOME; FAMILY; HEARTH & HOME
HOUSE & RING	LEASE OR CONTRACT SIGNED; FAMILY NAME; HOUSEHOLD
HOUSE & BOOK	PUBLISHING HOUSE; SECRET ROOMS; FAMILY SECRET; LIBRARY
HOUSE & LETTER	HOUSE DOCUMENTS; DEEDS; FAMILY DOCUMENTS
HOUSE & MAN	HOMEOWNER; LANDLORD; MAN'S HOME
HOUSE & WOMAN	HOMEOWNER; LANDLADY; WOMAN'S HOME
HOUSE & LILY	OLD HOUSE; ESTABLISHED FAMILY
HOUSE & SUN	SUCCESS AT HOME; HIGH-ACHIEVING FAMILY
HOUSE & MOON	FANTASY HOME; CREATIVE PLACE; EMOTIONAL FAMILY
HOUSE & KEY	IMPORTANT HOUSE; SPIRITUAL HOMECOMING
HOUSE & FISH	HOME-BASED BUSINESS; ESTATE AGENT; BRAND
HOUSE & ANCHOR	LONG-TERM SECURITY; COMMITTED FAMILY
HOUSE & CROSS	CHURCH; HOUSE WITH NEGATIVE HISTORY

5. TREE

Playing Card:	**Seven of Hearts**
General (Noun):	Health, Wellbeing, Vitality, Energy, Growth, Spirituality, Karma
General (Adj):	Healthy, Well, Energetic, Growing, Vital, Karmic, Spiritual, Lush
Love:	Flourishing Love Life, Budding Relationship, Karmic Return
Career:	Healthy Growth, Branching Out, Career Vitality, Healthcare
People:	Energetic, Health-Conscious, Shamanic, Spiritual
Timing:	May. Five Days, Weeks, Months. Fifth of the Month

Card's Message

Keep yourself strong and healthy - inside and out, mind, body, spirit. Keep an eye out for health problems, read the signs. Take a holistic approach. A time of energy and wellbeing - take care of yourself.

Tree Card Combinations

TREE & RIDER: GOOD HEALTH ON ITS WAY; HEALTH NEWS; KARMA

TREE & CLOVER: LUCKY KARMA; GOOD HEALTH; FORTUNATE DEVELOPMENT

TREE & SHIP: HEALTH-RELATED TRIP; SPIRITUAL JOURNEY

TREE & HOUSE: FAMILY HEALTH; HEALTH SPA; STRUCTURAL HEALTH

TREE & CLOUDS: UNDER THE WEATHER; MYSTERY AILMENT; HEALTH ISSUE

TREE & SNAKE: SICKNESS, BUG; STOMACH PROBLEM; SEXUAL FUNCTION

TREE & COFFIN: SERIOUS ILLNESS; DECLINING HEALTH; DEPRESSION

TREE & BOUQUET: FLOURISHING; HEALTH & WELLBEING; IMPROVEMENTS

TREE & SCYTHE: SUDDEN ILLNESS; SURGERY; REDUCED VITALITY

TREE & WHIP: SEXUAL HEALTH; SPORTS INJURY; MUSCLE STRAIN

TREE & BIRDS: THERAPY; VOICE PROBLEMS; VOCAL HEALTH

TREE & CHILD: PREGNANCY; CHILDHOOD ILLNESS; SMALL HEALTH ISSUE

TREE & FOX: UNDISCOVERED HEALTH PROBLEM; OCCUPATIONAL HEALTH

TREE & BEAR: WEIGHT ISSUES; DIETARY HEALTH; FINANCIAL HEALTH OR GROWTH

TREE & STARS: RECOVERY; EXCELLENT HEALTH; HEALING; HEALTH GOALS

TREE & STORKS: BOUNCING BACK; NEW LEASE OF LIFE; NEW LIFESTYLE; BIRTH

TREE & DOG: SOULMATE; DEEP FRIENDSHIP; HOLISTIC HEALTH

TREE & TOWER: HOSPITAL, CLINIC, HEALTH CENTRE; ORGANISATIONAL HEALTH

TREE & GARDEN:	SPA; PUBLIC HEALTH; OUTDOOR ACTIVITIES
TREE & MOUNTAIN:	BLOCKAGE; EXHAUSTION, FEELING SLUGGISH
TREE & CROSSROAD:	DIFFERENT TREATMENT OPTIONS; SPIRITUAL CHOICES
TREE & MICE:	STRESS, ANXIETY; HEALTH WORRIES; HYPOCHONDRIA
TREE & HEART:	HEART TROUBLE; RELATIONSHIP HEALTH; OLD LOVE
TREE & RING:	MARRIAGE HEALTH: KARMIC BOND: RECURRING HEALTH ISSUE
TREE & BOOK:	CHECK-UP; HIDDEN HEALTH ISSUE; RESEARCHING SYMPTOMS
TREE & LETTER:	HEALTH CERTIFICATE; DOCTOR'S NOTE; PRESCRIPTION
TREE & MAN:	MAN'S HEALTH; HEALER; PAST LIFE CONNECTION
TREE & WOMAN:	WOMAN'S HEALTH; HEALER, PAST LIFE CONNECTION
TREE & LILY:	AGEING HEALTH ISSUES; HEALTH IN SENIOR YEARS
TREE & SUN:	EXCELLENT HEALTH; RECOVERY; SUN-SCREEN
TREE & MOON:	EMOTIONAL HEALTH; HORMONE ISSUES
TREE & KEY:	KARMA; LIFE PURPOSE; LIFE LESSON; VITALITY
TREE & FISH:	FERTILITY; LIVING UNASSISTED; BUSINESS HEALTH
TREE & ANCHOR:	LONG-TERM HEALTH AND WELLBEING; LASTING VITALITY
TREE & CROSS:	DEPRESSION; CHRONIC HEALTH ISSUES

6. CLOUDS

Playing Card:	**King of Clubs**
General (Noun):	Uncertainty, Confusion, Doubt, Instability, Bad Weather, Fog
General (Adj):	Confused, Unclear, Dark, Obscured, Unstable, Misty, Vague
Love:	Unclear Relationship, Moodiness, Confusing Relationship
Career:	Lack of Concrete Info, Unclear People, Deals, Situation
People:	Flaky, Vague, Confused, Distracted, Hard To Pin Down, Illogical
Timing:	June, Six months, Weeks, Days, Sixth of the Month

Card's Message

Doubts prevail; something isn't clear or is being obscured from you, or is overshadowing things. Try to pin down the details and clear your mind. Watch for what's being hidden.

CLOUDS CARD COMBINATIONS

CLOUDS & RIDER: CONFUSING OR BAD TIMES COMING; UNCLEAR MESSAGE

CLOUDS & CLOVER: HAPPY OBLIVION; STUMBLING INTO LUCKY CIRCUMSTANCES

CLOUDS & SHIP: UNCERTAIN OR UNCLEAR JOURNEY

CLOUDS & HOUSE; UNCERTAIN LIVING CIRCUMSTANCES; HOUSE SALE PROBLEMS

CLOUDS & TREE: VAGUE SYMPTOMS; HEALTH UNCERTAINTY: MENTAL HEALTH

CLOUDS & SNAKE: COMPLICATIONS; SNAKE OIL; DELIBERATE CONFUSION

CLOUDS & COFFIN: CLARITY; RESOLUTION; PROBLEMS END; GRIEF SYMPTOMS

CLOUDS & BOUQUET: DREAMS; DAYDREAMS; HAPPILY TIPSY

CLOUDS & SCYTHE: CUT THROUGH CONFUSION; SHARPNESS; BAD DECISIONS

CLOUDS & WHIP: GASLIGHTING; ABUSE; BLURRING OF SEXUAL BOUNDARIES

CLOUDS & BIRDS: MISCOMMUNICATION; MISUNDERSTANDING; RUMOUR

CLOUDS & CHILD: CHILDLIKE CONFUSION; SMALL MISUNDERSTANDING

CLOUDS & FOX CORRUPTION; MANIPULATION; JOB UNCERTAINTY

CLOUDS & BEAR: MONEY ISSUES; POOR MANAGER; UNCERTAIN FINANCES

CLOUDS & STARS: FANTASIES; LAZINESS; DELUSIONS OF GRANDEUR

CLOUDS & STORKS: STEP INTO THE UNKNOWN; UNCERTAIN CHANGE

CLOUDS & DOG: DISLOYALTY; UNTRUSTWORTHY FRIEND; BETRAYAL

CLOUDS & TOWER:	SHADY CORPORATION; MURKY OFFICIALDOM; COVERUP
CLOUDS & GARDEN:	EVENT MARRED; NETWORKING ISSUES
CLOUDS & MOUNTAIN:	WARNING; RED FLAGS; DELAYS AND CONFUSION
CLOUDS & CROSSROAD:	CHOICES OBSCURED; PATH UNCERTAIN
CLOUDS & MICE:	ANXIOUS CONFUSION; WORRIES; DEMENTIA; FEAR
CLOUDS & HEART:	CHEATING; UNCERTAIN ROMANCE
CLOUDS & RING:	MARRIAGE PROBLEMS; HIDDEN MARRIAGE; DODGY DEAL
CLOUDS & BOOK:	SECRETS; HIDDEN KNOWLEDGE; PLAGIARISM
CLOUDS & LETTER:	FORGERY; FAKE NEWS; LACK OF WRITTEN CLARITY
CLOUDS & MAN:	CONMAN; UNSTABLE MAN; MAN'S UNCERTAINTY
CLOUDS & WOMAN:	CON-WOMAN; UNSTABLE WOMAN; WOMAN'S UNCERTAINTY
CLOUDS & LILY:	DEMENTIA; MEMORY PROBLEMS; OLD AGE FORGETFULNESS
CLOUDS & SUN:	VICTORY IN THE END; ALL COMES GOOD
CLOUDS & MOON:	EMOTIONAL CONFUSION; MOODINESS
CLOUDS & KEY:	RESOLUTION; THE ANSWER IS FOUND
CLOUDS & FISH:	DODGY BUSINESS PRACTICES; BUSINESS UNCERTAINTY
CLOUDS & ANCHOR:	LONG-TERM UNCERTAINTY; STABILITY IN CONFUSION
CLOUDS & CROSS:	DESPAIR, HOPELESSNESS; DEMENTIA

7. SNAKE

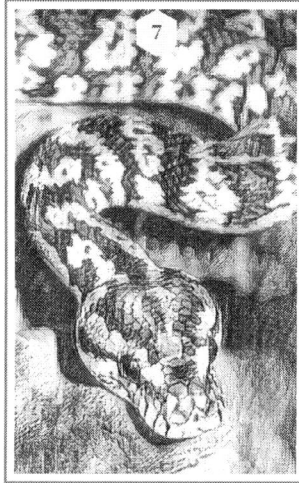

Playing Card:	**Queen of Clubs**
General (Noun):	Betrayal, Negativity, Problem, Threat, Treachery, Misfortune
General (Adj):	Bad, Negative, Corrupt, Betraying, Unlucky, Jealous, Seductive
Love:	Cheat Untrustworthy, Love-Rat. Temptress. Seducer.
Career:	Problems. Undermining. Check the Small Print
People:	Double Crosser, Cheat, Liar, Snake-In-The-Grass.
Timing:	July, Seven Days, Weeks, Months. Seventh of the Month.

Card's Message

A warning of problems or someone who cannot be trusted. Can you spot them? Don't ignore your instincts or any bad vibes you get. Watch your back. The faster you can spot problems, the faster they can be dealt with—and put out of your life.

SNAKE CARD COMBINATIONS

SNAKE & RIDER: HELP COMING; DISHONEST NEWS; LIES

SNAKE & CLOVER: SOLUTION; REPAIRS; LUCKY WOMAN

SNAKE & SHIP: TRAVEL PROBLEMS; TRIP WITH A LIAR

SNAKE & HOUSE: UNTRUSTWORTHY FAMILY; DOMESTIC PROBLEMS

SNAKE & TREE: HEALTH PROBLEMS; HEALTHY CYNICISM

SNAKE & CLOUDS: CONFUSION; GASLIGHTING; NO SOLUTION

SNAKE & COFFIN: PROBLEMS ENDING; TERMINAL PROBLEM

SNAKE & BOUQUET: POSITIVE RESOLUTION; SILVER LINING

SNAKE & SCYTHE: SURGERY, RECOVERY; SWIFT REMOVAL OF PROBLEM

SNAKE & WHIP: ABUSE, SEXUAL ABUSE; INJURY; PROMISCUITY

SNAKE & BIRDS: NEGATIVE GOSSIP, SLANDER; DIFFICULT NEGOTIATIONS

SNAKE & CHILD: DIFFICULT OR PROBLEM CHILD; CHILDISH BETRAYER

SNAKE & FOX: WORK PROBLEMS; UNTRUSTWORTHY EMPLOYEE; WORK RIVAL

SNAKE & BEAR: MONEY TROUBLES; BAD MANAGER; CONTROL FREAK

SNAKE & STARS: DIFFICULT PROJECT; CHALLENGING HIGH-FLYER;

SNAKE & STORKS: RISKY MOVE; DIFFICULT NEW START; FALSE START

SNAKE & DOG: UNTRUSTWORTHY FRIEND; WRONG ADVICE

SNAKE & TOWER: HIGH-LEVEL CORRUPTION; LAWSUIT

SNAKE & GARDEN:	UNTRUSTWORTHY SOCIAL CONNECTION; DIFFICULT EVENT
SNAKE & MOUNTAIN:	BIG BLOCKS; UNRESOLVED TROUBLES; TROUBLES PREVENTED
SNAKE & CROSSROAD:	MULTIPLE DECEPTIONS; RUNNING AWAY FROM PROBLEMS
SNAKE & MICE:	MAJOR PROBLEMS; ANXIETY; THINGS GET WORSE
SNAKE & HEART:	ROMANTIC BETRAYAL; CHEATING; SEDUCTION
SNAKE & RING:	BROKEN CONTRACT; RELATIONSHIP PROBLEMS; BAD DEAL
SNAKE & BOOK:	SECRET BETRAYAL; HIDDEN PROBLEMS; UNPLEASANT SECRETS
SNAKE & LETTER:	BAD NEWS; NEGATIVE REVIEW; FAKE NEWS
SNAKE & MAN:	CONMAN; CHEATING MAN; UNTRUSTWORTHY MAN
SNAKE & WOMAN:	FEMALE CON ARTIST; CHEAT; UNTRUSTWORTHY WOMAN
SNAKE & LILY:	CHEATING OLDER MAN; AGEING PROBLEMS
SNAKE & SUN:	SUCCESS AFTER DIFFICULTIES; COSTLY SUCCESS
SNAKE & MOON:	EMOTIONAL PROBLEMS; BAD MOODS; ILLUSIONS
SNAKE & KEY:	SOLUTION; SUCCESS AFTER BETRAYAL; DODGING A BULLET
SNAKE & FISH:	BUSINESS TROUBLES; FRAUD; THREAT TO INDEPENDENCE
SNAKE & ANCHOR:	LONG-TERM PROBLEMS; INSECURITY; INSTABILITY
SNAKE & CROSS:	BIG PROBLEMS; SUFFERING; BETRAYAL; GUILT

8. COFFIN

Playing Card:	**Nine of Diamonds**
General (Noun):	Death, End, Major Loss, Finale, Defeat, Dread, Closure, Funeral
General (Adj):	Dying, Last, Finished, Final, Ending, Closing
Love:	Relationship End, Closure, Mourning, Dying Love, Widowhood
Career:	Job Loss, Work Ends, Undertaker, Mortuary, Dead-End
People:	Ill Individual, Depressed, Down, Negative Person, Misery
Timing:	August, Eight Days, Weeks Months, Eighth of the Month

Card's Message

Something big is coming to an end, and probably unavoidable. It may be painful and involve a process of mourning, but it's only when the past is finally left behind that transformation can occur. Out with the old, in with the new.

COFFIN CARD COMBINATIONS

COFFIN & RIDER: ENDING, BIG CHANGE COMING

COFFIN & CLOVER: LUCKY ENDING; SECOND CHANCE

COFFIN & SHIP: MOVING AWAY; EMIGRATION; DEATH

COFFIN & HOUSE: HOUSE MOVE; RESTRUCTURE; FAMILY TOMB

COFFIN & TREE: ILLNESS; DEPRESSION; SPIRITUAL ENDING

COFFIN & CLOUDS: MENTAL ILLNESS; NERVOUS BREAKDOWN

COFFIN & SNAKE: BIG PROBLEMS; DIFFICULT ENDING

COFFIN & BOUQUET: RECOVERY; FUNERAL; HAPPY ENDING

COFFIN & SCYTHE: ACCIDENT; TROUBLES END; BAD DECISIONS

COFFIN & WHIP: ABUSE; VIOLENCE; DESTRUCTION

COFFIN & BIRDS: COMMUNICATION ENDS; NEGATIVE CONVERSATION

COFFIN & CHILD: DESTRUCTIVE CHILD; NEW START AFTER PROBLEMS

COFFIN & FOX: JOB LOSS; DECEIT ENDS

COFFIN & BEAR: INHERITANCE; FINANCIAL CHANGES

COFFIN & STARS: HOPE; RELIEF; IMPROVEMENTS; POSITIVE ENDING

COFFIN & STORKS: LETTING GO; NEGATIVE CHANGE

COFFIN & DOG: FRIEND IN NEED; FRIENDSHIP ENDS

COFFIN & TOWER: CORPORATE END; OFFICIAL ENDING; PRISON; MORGUE

COFFIN & GARDEN:	FUNERAL; CEMETERY; CANCELLED EVENT
COFFIN & MOUNTAIN:	STUCK; ISOLATION; LACK OF MOVEMENT
COFFIN & CROSSROAD:	NEW DIRECTION; CHOICE OF ENDINGS
COFFIN & MICE:	FEARS, WORRIES; ANXIOUS DEPRESSION
COFFIN & HEART:	GRIEF; HEARTACHE; END OF ROMANCE
COFFIN & RING:	MARRIAGE ENDING; RELATIONSHIP OVER; CONTRACT ENDS
COFFIN & BOOK:	SECRET REVEALED; AUTOPSY
COFFIN & LETTER:	OBITUARY; WILL; RESIGNATION LETTER; CANCELLATION
COFFIN & MAN:	ILL OR DEPRESSED MAN; MALE ENDING
COFFIN & WOMAN:	ILL OR DEPRESSED WOMAN; FEMALE ENDING
COFFIN & LILY:	OLD AGE; DYING; MATURE ENDING
COFFIN & SUN:	SECOND CHANCE; SUCCESS IN THE END
COFFIN & MOON:	SHOCK; EMOTIONAL ENDING; GRIEF
COFFIN & KEY:	KARMA; A LIFE-CHANGER; NECESSARY ENDING
COFFIN & FISH:	FUNERAL BUSINESS; BUSINESS FAILURE; LOSS OF MONEY
COFFIN & ANCHOR:	LONG-TERM TROUBLES; LONGING
COFFIN & CROSS:	PAIN; GRIEF; SERIOUS DEPRESSION

9. BOUQUET

Playing Card:	**Queen of Spades**
General (Noun):	Beauty, Loveliness, Blossom, Pleasantness, Gift, Blessing
General (Adj):	Good-Looking, Handsome, Pleasant, Lovely, Blossoming
Love:	Joy, Wedding, Pleasure, Gifts, Delight, Blossoming Romance
Career:	Honour, Fruits of One's Labour, Florist, Beauty Industry
People:	Attractive, Agreeable, Artistic, Design or Fashion-Conscious
Timing:	September, Nine Days, Weeks, Months. Ninth of the Month.

Card's Message

Good times! Abundance and beauty awaits. Positivity is all around, and pleasantries. Enjoy the good things in life, however small. Look for blessings and gifts.

Bouquet Card Combinations

BOUQUET & RIDER: GIFT; PLEASANT VISITOR; POSITIVE ENCOUNTER

BOUQUET & CLOVER: JOY; GOOD LUCK; SURPRISE GIFT

BOUQUET & SHIP: PLEASANT TRIP; LOVELY HOLIDAY

BOUQUET & HOUSE: HOME DECORATING; BEAUTIFUL HOUSE; PLEASANT HOME;

BOUQUET & TREE: BLOOMING HEALTH; NATURE

BOUQUET & CLOUDS: DAYDREAMS; PLEASANT FANTASIES; LAZINESS

BOUQUET & SNAKE: TEMPTING BEAUTY; ALL THAT GLITTERS; JEALOUSY

BOUQUET & COFFIN: FUNERAL FLOWERS; DISAPPOINTMENT, LET-DOWN

BOUQUET & SCYTHE: PLASTIC SURGERY; POSITIVE DECISION

BOUQUET & WHIP: SEXUAL PLEASURE; ENDORPHINS; DANCING

BOUQUET & BIRDS: PLEASANT CONVERSATION; GOOD-LOOKING COUPLE

BOUQUET & CHILD: CHILDLIKE PLEASURE; SMALL PLEASURES; ATTRACTIVE CHILD

BOUQUET & FOX: WORK GIFT; BEAUTY JOB; FLORIST; FEIGNED POSITIVITY

BOUQUET & BEAR: FINANCIAL GIFT; GOOD FINANCIAL SITUATION

BOUQUET & STARS: ACCOLADE, RECOGNITION; DREAMS COME TRUE

BOUQUET & STORKS: POSITIVE NEW BEGINNING; HAPPY ARRIVAL; PROGRESS

BOUQUET & DOG: GOOD FRIENDSHIP; LOVELY FRIEND

BOUQUET & TOWER: BEAUTY AND FASHION INDUSTRY; SHOPPING MALL

BOUQUET & GARDEN: PARTY; GARDEN; HAPPY EVENT; PARK; LANDSCAPE

BOUQUET & MOUNTAIN: DELAYED PLEASURE; HIKING; OUTDOORS

BOUQUET & CROSSROAD: POSITIVE OPPORTUNITIES; MULTIPLE BLESSINGS

BOUQUET & MICE: BUTTERFLIES; ANTICIPATION; HAPPINESS SHORT-LIVED

BOUQUET & HEART: LOVE BLESSING; POSITIVE LOVE RELATIONSHIP

BOUQUET & RING: GOOD CONTRACT; HAPPY MARRIAGE

BOUQUET & BOOK: SECRET GIFT; LEARNING SOMETHING PLEASANT; BOOK PRIZE

BOUQUET & LETTER: GIFT DELIVERY; GOOD NEWS; INVITATION

BOUQUET & MAN: MALE CHARM; HANDSOME; GENTLEMAN

BOUQUET & WOMAN: FEMALE CHARM; BEAUTY; LADYLIKE

BOUQUET & LILY: SERENITY; PEACE; WISDOM; ACCEPTANCE; BLESSINGS OF EXPERIENCE

BOUQUET & SUN: GREAT SUCCESS; WIN; CELEBRATION

BOUQUET & MOON: ROMANTIC HAPPINESS; CREATIVE BLOSSOMING; FULFILMENT

BOUQUET & KEY: SIGNIFICANT BLESSING; GREAT SUCCESS; VERY BEAUTIFUL

BOUQUET & FISH: THRIVING BUSINESS; BEAUTY INDUSTRY

BOUQUET & ANCHOR: LONG TERM POSITIVITY; HAPPINESS; GOALS REACHED

BOUQUET & CROSS: CHARITY; BURDENED HAPPINESS; LOADED GIFT

10. SCYTHE

Playing Card	**Jack of Diamonds**
General (Noun)	Cut, Decision, Accident, Reduction, Surgery, Knife, Shock
General (Adj)	Sudden, Decisive, Hurtful, Reducing, Cutting, Dangerous,
Love	Breakup, Split, Divorce. Rejection. Going Separate Ways
Career	Redundancy, Broken agreements, Cutbacks, Tight Budgets
People	Decisive, Brutal, Critical, Cut-throat, No Niceties, Edgy
Timing:	October, Ten Days, Months, Weeks, Tenth of the Month

Card's Message

There's a need for care, clarity and precision. Be quick and decisive; get on with it, do what needs to be done. Possible splits or reductions in the air. There may be a risk of sudden accidents at this time; be sensible and take care.

Scythe Card Combinations

Scythe & Rider: SUDDEN DECISION; UNEXPECTED NEWS

Scythe & Clover: LUCKY DECISION; GOOD RESULTS

Scythe & Ship: JOURNEY ABRUPTLY ENDED; ACCIDENT; TRIP CUT SHORT

Scythe & House: DECISION ABOUT HOUSE; DAMAGED HOME; HOMELESS

Scythe & Tree: SURGERY; HEALTH DECISION; TREE FELLED

Scythe & Clouds: INDECISION; BAD DECISION; UNCLEAR OUTCOME

Scythe & Snake: BAD DECISION; ATTACK PHYSICAL HARM

Scythe & Coffin: FINALITY, FINAL DECISION; VIOLENCE; HARM

Scythe & Bouquet: POSITIVE DECISION; PROBLEMS RESOLVED

Scythe & Whip: TOUGH DECISION; ELIMINATION ROUND; WEAPONS

Scythe & Birds: BREAK-UP; VERBAL BREVITY; ARGUMENTS; VICIOUSNESS

Scythe & Child: CHILDHOOD ACCIDENT; GROWING UP SUDDENLY

Scythe & Fox: JOB CUTS; JOB LOSS; WORK DECISION

Scythe & Bear: FINANCIAL LOSSES; POWER REMOVED; DIET

Scythe & Stars: CUT DOWN TO SIZE; DIMINISHED; POSITIVE DECISION

Scythe & Storks: MOVING ON QUICKLY; FALSE START;

Scythe & Dog: EXILE; END OF FRIENDSHIP; LETTING GO

Scythe & Tower: EMERGENCY ROOM; FALL OF OFFICIAL BODY; GOVT CUTS

SCYTHE & GARDEN:	ISOLATED, OSTRACISED: GARDENING: CANCELLATION
SCYTHE & MOUNTAIN:	DECISION DELAYED OR BLOCKED; INCOMPLETE
SCYTHE & CROSSROAD:	MULTIPLE CHOICES; FINAL DECISION; SUDDEN DECISION
SCYTHE & MICE:	STRESSFUL DECISION; POOR CHOICE
SCYTHE & HEART:	LOVE SPLIT; HEARTBREAK; RELATIONSHIP DECISION
SCYTHE & RING:	DIVORCE; SEPARATION; BROKEN AGREEMENT; CUT TIES
SCYTHE & BOOK:	SECRET UNCOVERED; DISCOVERY
SCYTHE & LETTER:	CENSORSHIP; EDITING; DIVORCE PAPERS; HURTFUL NEWS
SCYTHE & MAN:	DECISIVE MAN; SURGEON; JUDGMENTAL MAN
SCYTHE & WOMAN:	DECISIVE WOMAN; SURGEON; JUDGMENTAL WOMAN
SCYTHE & LILY:	SUDDEN RETIREMENT; MATURE DECISION
SCYTHE & SUN:	SUCCESSFUL DECISION; GOOD RESULTS
SCYTHE & MOON:	ROMANTIC SPLIT; CREATIVE DECISION; SUDDEN INSIGHT
SCYTHE & KEY:	DECISIVE MOMENT; KEY TURNING-POINT; FATE
SCYTHE & FISH:	BUSINESS DECISION; FINANCIAL DECISION
SCYTHE & ANCHOR:	LONG TERM DECISION; NO TURNING BACK
SCYTHE & CROSS:	PAINFUL DECISION; SUFFERING; SELF-HARM

11. WHIP

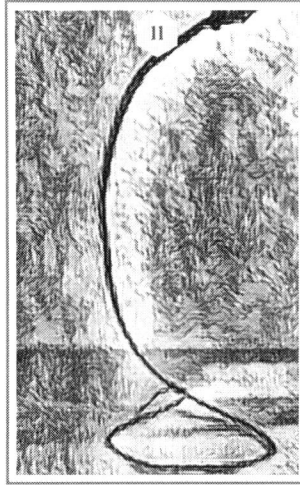

Playing Card	**Jack of Clubs**
General (Noun)	Hardship, Struggle, Abuse, Training, Sex, Conflict, Sport
General (Adj)	Abusive, Harsh, Argumentative, Sexual, Competitive, Avenging
Love	Sexuality, Physicality, Rows, Abuse, Conflict. Tempestuous.
Career	Hard Work, Training, Struggle, Discipline, Sportsperson, Gym
People	Harsh, Punitive, Argumentative, Feisty, Sporty, Disciplinarian
Timing:	November, Eleven Days, Weeks, Months, Eleventh of the Month

Card's Message

Hard work is needed; push yourself, go that little bit further, discipline is required. Don't let it tip into abuse. An argumentative atmosphere, you may have to fight and struggle to get what you want. Competition is high at this time.

WHIP CARD COMBINATIONS

WHIP & RIDER: HARSH FEEDBACK; ABUSE; REVENGE; CRITICISM

WHIP & CLOVER: GOOD SEX; HARD WORK GETS RESULTS; GAMBLING

WHIP & SHIP   BUMPY RIDE; DIFFICULT JOURNEY; SPORTS TRIP

WHIP & HOUSE: DOMESTIC ABUSE; HOME GYM

WHIP & TREE: HEALTH PROBLEMS; NEGATIVE KARMA; INJURY

WHIP & CLOUDS: PSYCHOLOGICAL ABUSE; DEMENTIA; CONFUSED SEXUALITY;

WHIP & SNAKE: TROUBLEMAKER; FEMALE SEXUALITY; DANGER

WHIP & COFFIN: SERIOUS HARM; END OF ABUSE; DESTRUCTION

WHIP & BOUQUET: PLEASURABLE SEX; EXERCISE HIGH

WHIP & SCYTHE: VIOLENCE; B.D.S.M; ACCIDENT

WHIP & BIRDS: PHONE SEX; TOUGH DEBATE; VERBAL ABUSE; ARGUMENT

WHIP & CHILD: TRAINING, COACHING, KIDS' SPORTS; ACTIVE CHILD

WHIP & FOX;   HARD WORK; SURVIVAL; MILITARY; WORKPLACE BULLYING

WHIP & BEAR;   FINANCIAL STRUGGLES; PERSONAL TRAINER; BODYBUILDING

WHIP & STARS: TRAINING TO BE THE BEST; COACHING

WHIP & STORKS: TOUGH NEW START; DIFFICULT AT THE BEGINNING; INITIAL EFFORT

WHIP & DOG: FRIENDS WITH BENEFITS; TEASING; PERSONAL TRAINER

WHIP & TOWER: GYM; LEGAL OR OFFICIAL DIFFICULTIES; FORTRESS

WHIP & GARDEN: GROUP BULLYING; PEER PRESSURE; PUBLIC ARGUMENT

WHIP & MOUNTAIN: MOUNTAIN-CLIMBING; SAFEGUARDING; LIMITATION; HARD WORK

WHIP & CROSSROAD: DIFFICULT CHOICES; UNSETTLED; MULTIPLE ABUSES

WHIP & MICE: ANXIETY; EXHAUSTION; STRESS

WHIP & HEART: SEX; HEARTBREAK; LOVE CONFLICT

WHIP & RING: DIFFICULT OR ABUSIVE RELATIONSHIP; HARSH CONTRACT

WHIP & BOOK: HIDDEN SEXUALITY; HIDDEN ABUSE; ACADEMIC HARD WORK

WHIP & LETTER: EROTIC FICTION; ABUSIVE MESSAGE, THREAT

WHIP & MAN: MALE SEXUALITY; MALE ABUSER; FIT MAN; CRITIC

WHIP & WOMAN: FEMALE SEXUALITY; FEMALE ABUSER; FIT WOMAN; CRITIC

WHIP & LILY: AGEING TROUBLES; OLD AGE HARDSHIP; MATURE SEXUALITY

WHIP & SUN: HARD WORK BRINGS SUCCESS; CHARISMA; VICTORY

WHIP & MOON: EMOTIONAL ABUSE; DEPRESSION; OBSESSION; SEDUCTION

WHIP & KEY: IMPORTANT LIFE LESSON; NECESSARY ACTION

WHIP & FISH: BUSINESS DIFFICULTIES; MONEY FIGHTS; HARD WORK

WHIP & ANCHOR: LONG-TERM HARDSHIP; CONSISTENT EFFORT

WHIP & CROSS: SEVERE DEPRESSION; GUILT; SELF-FLAGELLATION

12. BIRDS

Playing Card	**Seven of Diamonds**
General (Noun)	Talk, Speech, Debate, Conversation, Communication, Speech,
General (Adj)	Verbal, Communicative, Discussed, Debated, Spoken
Love	Lovebirds, Pairing, Good Communication, Chat, Phone Calls
Career:	Talks, Meetings, Negotiation, Presentation, Communications
People:	Communicators, Storytellers, Chatty, PR people, Articulate
Timing:	December, Twelve Days, Months, a Year, Annual, Twelfth

Card's Message

Communication is all. Who do you need to connect with? Meet, ask questions, listen, discuss. Negotiate if you need to - it's time to sit down and talk.

BIRDS CARD COMBINATIONS

BIRDS & RIDER: DELIVERY OF MESSAGES; RESPONSE; DISCUSSIONS

BIRDS & CLOVER: CHANCE CONVERSATION; LUCKY COMMUNICATION

BIRDS & SHIP: OVERSEAS NEGOTIATION; TALKING ABOUT A TRIP

BIRDS & HOUSE: DOMESTIC DISCUSSIONS; HOUSE NEGOTIATIONS; FLATMATES

BIRDS & TREE   HEALTH DISCUSSION; KARMIC CONVERSATION

BIRDS & CLOUDS: MIXED MESSAGES; MISCOMMUNICATION

BIRDS & SNAKE: DECEITFUL CONVERSATION; BEING BUTTERED UP; GOSSIP

BIRDS & COFFIN: FINAL COMMUNICATION; COMMUNICATION ENDS; SILENCE

BIRDS & BOUQUET: LOVEBIRDS; PLEASANT CONVERSATION

BIRDS & SCYTHE: CUTTING OFF COMMUNICATION; SPLIT

BIRDS & WHIP: SEX-TALK; CHALLENGING CONVERSATION; ARGUMENTS

BIRDS & CHILD: TALKING ABOUT PREGNANCY; BEGINNER'S TALK; KIDS' CHAT

BIRDS & FOX: WORK CONVERSATION; DECEPTIVE CONVERSATION

BIRDS & BEAR: FINANCIAL TALKS; MANAGER'S MEETING; MONEY TALK

BIRDS & STARS: STAR INTERVIEW; PROMISING CHAT

BIRDS & STORKS: INTRODUCTORY TALK; FRESH COMMUNICATION;

BIRDS & DOG: CONVERSATION WITH A FRIEND; FRIENDLY ADVICE

BIRDS & TOWER:	MEDIA ORGANIZATION; OFFICIAL COMMS; LEGAL DISCUSSION
BIRDS & GARDEN:	PUBLIC DISCUSSION; SOCIAL MEDIA; PUBLIC SPEAKING
BIRDS & MOUNTAIN:	COMMUNICATION DELAYS; BLOCKED COMMUNICATION
BIRDS & CROSSROAD:	MULTIPLE DISCUSSIONS; CHOICE OF COMMUNICATION; SPLIT
BIRDS & MICE:	ANXIOUS COUPLE; WORRIED COMMUNICATION
BIRDS & HEART:	LOVE BIRDS; ROMANTIC TALK; PASSIONATE CONVERSATION
BIRDS & RING:	PROPOSAL; DEALINGS; NEGOTIATIONS; AGREEMENT
BIRDS & BOOK:	SECRET CONVERSATION; SEMINAR; TEACHING
BIRDS & LETTER:	WRITTEN COMMUNICATION; MESSAGE; EMAIL
BIRDS & MAN:	MAN'S CONVERSATION; MALE COMMUNICATOR
BIRDS & WOMAN:	FEMALE CONVERSATION; FEMALE COMMUNICATOR
BIRDS & LILY:	MATURE DISCUSSION; GROWN-UPS TALKING; WISE WORDS
BIRDS & SUN:	MOTIVATIONAL SPEAKING; SUCCESSFUL CONVERSATION
BIRDS & MOON:	EMOTIONAL CONVERSATION; CREATIVE MEETING
BIRDS & KEY:	SIGNIFICANT CONVERSATION; KEY COMMUNICATION
BIRDS & FISH:	BUSINESS MEETING; BUSINESS CONVERSATION; SALES PITCH
BIRDS & ANCHOR:	LONG-TERM DISCUSSION; MEETING; TOGETHERNESS
BIRDS & CROSS:	COUNSELLING; RELIGIOUS TALK; WEIGHTY CONVERSATION

13. CHILD

Playing Card	**Jack of Spades**
General (Noun):	Child, Young Person, Youth, Naivety, Innocence, Beginner
General (Adj):	Young, Immature, Childlike, Childish, Naive, Innocent, Small
Love:	Young Love; Childlike Innocence; Beginnings; Baby; Pregnancy
Career:	New Hire, Line Report, Junior, Working With Kids, Child-Care
People:	Youthful, Young, Naive, Childlike, Open, Physically Small, Teen
Timing:	Thirteen Days, Weeks, Months. Thirteenth of the Month

Card's Message

Let go and let yourself be playful for a bit. Be open to new experiences, as if you are seeing them for the first time. Do something just for fun, just for the pleasure of doing. Learn something new, try it out.

CHILD CARD COMBINATIONS

CHILD & RIDER: BIRTH ANNOUNCEMENT; NEW ARRIVAL

CHILD & CLOVER: LUCKY CHILD; BEGINNER'S LUCK; SMALL PIECE OF LUCK

CHILD & SHIP: TRIP WITH A CHILD; FOREIGN CHILD; SHORT TRIP

CHILD & HOUSE: FAMILY HOME; DOLL'S HOUSE; BABYSITTING

CHILD & TREE: GROWING CHILD; CHILDREN'S HEALTH; FERTILITY

CHILD & CLOUDS: CONFUSED CHILD; UNCLEAR BEGINNER

CHILD & SNAKE: UNTRUSTWORTHY KID; DIFFICULT CHILD; PROBLEM CHILD

CHILD & COFFIN: CHILDHOOD ENDS; ABANDONED CHILD; MISCARRIAGE

CHILD & BOUQUET: HAPPY CHILD; PLEASANT KID; ATTRACTIVE CHILD

CHILD & SCYTHE: CHILDHOOD ACCIDENT; DECISIVE KID; SURGERY

CHILD & WHIP: HARDWORKING CHILD; KID'S TRAINING; BULLY

CHILD & BIRDS: CHATTY KID; SIBLINGS; PLAYMATES

CHILD & FOX: SNEAKY KID; WORKING WITH CHILDREN; STARTER EMPLOYEE

CHILD & BEAR: OVERWEIGHT CHILD; FINANCIAL BEGINNER; STRONG CHILD

CHILD & STARS   GIFTED CHILD; EARLY HIGH ACHIEVER

CHILD & STORKS: BIRTH; NEW START FOR A CHILD; TOTAL BEGINNER

CHILD & DOG: FRIENDLY KID; CHILDHOOD FRIEND

CHILD & TOWER: SCHOOL; GOVERNING BODY; SOCIAL/CHILD SERVICES

CHILD & GARDEN: PLAYMATES; CLASS; SOCIABLE CHILD; PEER-GROUP; DAY-CARE

CHILD & MOUNTAIN: INFERTILITY; STRUGGLING CHILD; LONELY CHILD

CHILD & CROSSROAD: SEVERAL CHILDREN; TWINS; NEW PATH

CHILD & MICE: ANXIOUS OR NERVOUS CHILD

CHILD & HEART: LOVING KID; LOVECHILD; YOUNGER RIVAL

CHILD & RING: RELATIONSHIP WITH CHILD; ADOPTION

CHILD & BOOK   STUDENT, PUPIL; CLEVER CHILD; SCHOOL; SECRET CHILD

CHILD & LETTER: NEWS OF A BIRTH; MESSAGE FROM A CHILD

CHILD & MAN: CHILDISH MAN; MALE CHILD; MALE BEGINNER

CHILD & WOMAN: CHILDISH WOMAN; FEMALE CHILD; FEMALE BEGINNER

CHILD & LILY: OLD BEFORE THEIR TIME; ELDEST CHILD; MATURE BEGINNER

CHILD & SUN: SUCCESSFUL CHILD; HIGH ACHIEVER; HAPPY CHILD

CHILD & MOON: EMOTIONAL CHILD; CREATIVE KID

CHILD & KEY: IMPORTANT CHILD; SUCCESSFUL CHILD; HEIR

CHILD & FISH: BUSINESS BEGINNER; STARTUP; CHILD-RELATED BUSINESS

CHILD & ANCHOR: SETTLED CHILD; RESPONSIBLE CHILD

CHILD & CROSS: DEPRESSED CHILD; CHILDHOOD BURDEN

14. FOX

Playing Card	**Nine of Clubs**
General (Noun)	Work, Employment, Smarts, Survival, Cunning, Deceit
General (Adj)	Work-Related, Cunning, Deceitful, Stealthy, Shrewd
Love	Deceitful Person, Manipulation, Taking Advantage
Career:	Worker, Survivor, Put Food On The Table, Underhanded
People:	Deceptive, Manipulative, Players, Selfish, Worker, Grafter
Timing:	Fourteen Days, Weeks, Months, Fourteenth of the Month

Card's Message

Keep an eye out. Someone could be pulling the wool over your eyes, so be alert. Don't be over-trusting or give too much away. Have your wits about you at all times. It's everyone for themselves.

Fox Card Combinations

Fox & Rider: JOB OFFER; DOOR TO DOOR SALESMAN; NEW EMPLOYEE

Fox & Clover: CHANCER; OPPORTUNIST; PROMOTION; JOB OPPORTUNITY

Fox & Ship: TRAVEL FOR WORK; OVERSEAS EMPLOYEE; TRAVEL EMPLOYEE

Fox & House: HOMEWORKER; DOMESTIC WORKER; FAMILY DECEIVER

Fox & Tree: HEALTH-WORKER; DOCTOR; SPIRITUAL CHARLATAN

Fox & Clouds   JOB UNCERTAINTY; SOMEONE UNTRUSTWORTHY

Fox & Snake: CON ARTIST; BETRAYAL; DANGER

Fox & Coffin: JOB ENDS; LOSS OF EMPLOYMENT; MORTICIAN; UNDERTAKER

Fox & Bouquet: BEAUTY WORKER; PLEASANT JOB; NICE WORK; DECEPTIVE LOOKS

Fox & Scythe: REDUNDANCY; JOB LOSS; ACCIDENT AT WORK

Fox & Whip: HARSH JOB; TRAINING, COACHING

Fox & Birds: INTERVIEW; COMMUNICATIONS JOB; LYING

Fox & Child: JOB WITH CHILDREN; NEW EMPLOYEE; CUNNING CHILD

Fox & Bear: FINANCIAL JOB, ACCOUNTANCY; MANAGER; THEFT

Fox & Stars: STAR EMPLOYEE; ASTRONAUT; AGENT, PUBLIC RELATIONS

Fox & Storks   NEW JOB; JOB CHANGE; NEW START AT WORK

Fox & Dog: COLLEAGUES; DISHONEST FRIEND

FOX & TOWER	GOVERNMENT WORKER; PROFESSIONAL JOB; LAWYER;
FOX & GARDEN:	PUBLIC SECTOR WORKER; GARDENER; EVENTS WORK
FOX & MOUNTAIN:	UNEMPLOYMENT; BLOCKED WORK; MOUNTAINEER
FOX & CROSSROAD:	CAREER CHOICES; JOB OPTIONS; SMART DECISION
FOX & MICE:	WORK STRESS; JOB ANXIETY; JOB FEARS
FOX & HEART:	PASSIONATE WORK; ROMANTIC 'PLAYER'
FOX & RING:	CONTRACT WORK; JOB CONTRACT; DODGY CONTRACT
FOX & BOOK:	PUBLISHER; LIBRARIAN; INVESTIGATOR; ACADEMIC
FOX & LETTER:	WRITER; JOURNALIST; JOB NEWS; DECEPTIVE NEWS
FOX & MAN:	MALE EMPLOYEE; CON-MAN; MAN'S SURVIVAL
FOX & WOMAN:	FEMALE EMPLOYEE; CON-WOMAN; WOMAN'S SURVIVAL
FOX & LILY:	MATURE EMPLOYEE; EXPERIENCED WORKER
FOX & SUN:	SUCCESSFUL JOB-HUNT; SUCCESSFUL EMPLOYEE
FOX & MOON:	CREATIVE WORK, ARTS WORKER; EMOTIONAL JOB; PSYCHIC
FOX & KEY:	IMPORTANT JOB; KEY EMPLOYEE
FOX & FISH:	FREELANCING/FREELANCER; BUSINESS ADVISOR
FOX & ANCHOR:	STABLE JOB; LONG-TERM EMPLOYMENT
FOX & CROSS:	DEPRESSING WORK; PRESSURED JOB; CHARITY WORK

15. BEAR

Playing Card	**Ten of Clubs**
General (Noun)	Finances, Money, Power, Strength, Force, Weight, Protection,
General (Adj)	Financial, Powerful, Forceful, Strong, Muscular, Protective
Love	Protection, Wealthy lover, Strength. Nurturing, Overbearing
Career	Financial affairs, Wealth, Management, Power, Banking
People	Wealthy, Powerful people. Well-built, Muscular, Overweight.
Timing	Fifteen Days, Weeks, Months. Fifteenth of the Month.

Card's Message

Your financial life and prosperity. Have courage, have strength. Protection is either coming or you need to protect and stand up for yourself. Be fearless.

BEAR CARD COMBINATIONS

BEAR & RIDER: MONEY COMING: ARRIVAL OF POWERFUL VISITOR

BEAR & CLOVER: FINANCIAL GOOD FORTUNE; UNEXPECTED WINDFALL

BEAR & SHIP: OVERSEAS MONEY; MONEY TRANSFER; HOLIDAY MONEY

BEAR & HOUSE: DOMESTIC FINANCES: SALE MONEY:FAMILY INHERITANCE

BEAR & TREE: NUTRITION; BODY BUILDING; FINANCIAL HEALTH

BEAR & CLOUDS: FINANCIAL UNCERTAINTY; CONFUSED FINANCES

BEAR & SNAKE: FRAUD; FINANCIAL DECEPTION

BEAR & COFFIN: MONEY DRIES UP; POWER ENDING

BEAR & BOUQUET: POSITIVE FINANCIAL SITUATION; PROSPERITY; NICE BOSS

BEAR & SCYTHE: SUDDEN FINANCIAL LOSSES; FINANCIAL DECISION

BEAR & WHIP: GYM, TRAINING; FINANCIAL DIFFICULTIES; MONEY ROWS

BEAR & BIRDS: FINANCIAL DISCUSSION; TALKING ABOUT MONEY

BEAR & CHILD: CHILDHOOD OBESITY; FORCEFUL CHILD; TRUST FUND

BEAR & FOX: THEFT; FINANCIAL DECEPTION; SALARY

BEAR & STARS: FINANCIAL WIN; BONUS; CELEBRITY EARNINGS

BEAR & STORKS: FINANCIAL NEW BEGINNING; NEW DIET

BEAR & DOG: FINANCIAL HELP; LOAN; FRIENDLY BOSS; PERSONAL TRAINER

BEAR & TOWER: GOVERNMENT FINANCE; LEGAL FEES; TAXES; BANK

BEAR & GARDEN:	PUBLIC FINANCES; PUBLIC POWER; KITTY, PUBLIC 'POT'
BEAR & MOUNTAIN:	BLOCKED INCOME; MONEY DELAYS; PREVENTED POWER
BEAR & CROSSROAD:	MULTIPLE SOURCES OF INCOME; FINANCIAL CHOICES
BEAR & MICE:	MONEY WORRIES; FINANCIAL LOSSES; WORRYING POWER
BEAR & HEART:	PHILANTHROPY; FINANCIAL GENEROSITY
BEAR & RING:	FINANCIAL DEAL; MARITAL FINANCES; STRONG BOND
BEAR & BOOK:	SECRET STASH; ACADEMIC FUNDING; FINANCIAL SECRECY
BEAR & LETTER:	CASH; FINANCIAL DOCUMENTS; BANK STATEMENT;
BEAR & MAN:	BIG MAN; MALE PROTECTION; MAN'S FINANCES; BOSS
BEAR & WOMAN;	POWERFUL WOMAN; MAMA BEAR; WOMAN'S FINANCES; BOSS
BEAR & LILY:	EXPERIENCED BOSS; INHERITANCE; PENSION;
BEAR & SUN:	GOOD FINANCIAL SITUATION; FINANCIAL SUCCESS
BEAR & MOON:	EMOTIONAL OR CREATIVE POWER; CREATIVE FUNDING
BEAR & KEY:	FINANCES ARE KEY; IMPORTANT MONEY; FINANCIAL SUCCESS
BEAR & FISH:	BUSINESS FINANCES; ACCOUNTS
BEAR & ANCHOR:	SAVINGS; NEST-EGG; LONG-TERM POWER
BEAR & CROSS	FINANCIAL BURDEN; MONEY WORRIES; TRAPPINGS OF POWER

16. STARS

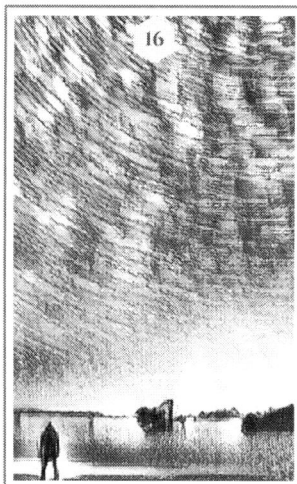

Playing Card	**Six of Hearts**
General (Noun)	Dreams, Goals, Ambitions, Achievements, Celebrity, Prize
General (Adj)	Ambitious, High-Achieving, Top, Star, Popular, Famous
Love:	Love Hopes & Dreams, Wishes, All You Desire
Career:	Ambitions, Goals, Achievements, High Performance
People:	Celebrity, High-Flier, Alpha, Diva, Ambitious, Big Picture
Timing:	Sixteen Days, Sixteenth of the Month, At Night

Card's Message

What are your hopes and dreams? Chart your ambitions and wishes; make a plan for how to get there, look for guidance. Believe in yourself and aim high.

Stars Card Combinations

STARS & RIDER:	DREAMS FULFILLED; ARRIVAL OF FAME; ACHIEVEMENT
STARS & CLOVER:	AMAZING LUCK; LUCKY STARS; PRIZE WIN
STAR & SHIP:	INTERNATIONAL FAME; DREAM TRIP; FOREIGN CELEB;
STARS & HOUSE:	DREAM HOME; WELL-KNOWN FAMILY; FAMOUS HOUSE
STARS & TREE:	DESTINY; PROMISING RECOVERY
STARS & CLOUDS:	FANTASIES; ILLUSIONS; DREAMS
STARS & SNAKE:	FEMALE SEX-SYMBOL; DREAMS BETRAYED
STARS & COFFIN:	END OF HOPES AND DREAMS; HOPES DASHED
STARS & BOUQUET:	AWARD; POSITIVE ACHIEVEMENT; ACCOLADES; FAME
STARS & SCYTHE:	SWIFT ACTION TOWARDS GOALS; DECISIVE ACHIEVEMENT
STARS & WHIP:	HARD-WORKING HIGH ACHIEVER; DIVA; SPORTSPERSON
STARS & BIRDS:	PUBLIC RELATIONS; NETWORKING; TOP-LEVEL TALKS
STARS & CHILD:	CHILD STAR; SPOILT CHILD; SUCCESSFUL BEGINNER
STARS & FOX:	STAR EMPLOYEE; BLAGGER; CELEBRITY PROMOTION
STARS & BEAR:	FINANCIAL GURU; MONEY GOALS; POWERFUL CELEB
STARS & STORKS:	HOPES OF A NEW BEGINNING; RISING STAR
STARS & DOG:	BEST FRIENDS; FAMOUS FRIENDS
STARS & TOWER:	A-LIST CELEB; ESTABLISHED STAR; REACHING FOR THE STARS

STARS & GARDEN:	WELL-CONNECTED; NATIONAL TREASURE; GLITTERING PARTY
STARS & MOUNTAIN:	BLOCKED DREAMS; HARD TO REACH GOALS
STARS & CROSSROAD:	CHOICE OF GOALS; SUCCESSFUL CHOICE
STARS & MICE:	STAGE FRIGHT; WORRIES ABOUT REPUTATION
STARS & HEART:	CRUSH; OBJECT OF AFFECTIONS
STARS & RING:	TOP RELATIONSHIP; MARRIAGE HOPES; CONTRACT GOALS
STARS & BOOK:	CHARACTERS; BESTSELLER; HIDDEN GOALS; ACADEMIC ACHIEVEMENT
STARS & LETTER:	GOOD NEWS; REFERENCE; CERTIFICATE
STARS & MAN:	MALE CELEB; POPULAR MAN; SUCCESSFUL MAN
STARS & WOMAN:	FEMALE CELEB; SUCCESSFUL WOMAN; POPULAR WOMAN
STARS & LILY:	LATE BLOOMER; OLDER CELEB
STARS & SUN:	HUGE SUCCESS; BIG ACHIEVEMENT; HONOUR
STARS & MOON:	CREATIVE GOALS; FAME; IDEAS
STARS & KEY:	WINNER; "THE ONE"; SIGNIFICANT GOALS; DESTINED FAME
STARS & FISH:	SUCCESSFUL ENTREPRENEUR; FINANCIAL GOALS
STARS & ANCHOR:	ESTABLISHED STAR; LEGENDARY
STARS & CROSS:	FATE; TROUBLED CELEB

17. STORKS

Playing Card	**Queen of Hearts**
General (Noun)	New Beginnings, Fresh Start, Renewal, Birth, Change
General (Adj)	Fresh, New, Revived, Newly Begun, Changed, Transformed
Love:	New Romance, Fresh Start, Next Step, Moving On, Birth
Career:	New Career, Starting Again, Start-Up, Change, Modernisation
People:	Progressives, Enterprise, Starts More Than Finishes
Timing:	Seventeen Days, Weeks, Seventeenth of the Month, Spring

Card's Message

Change and transformation coming into your life, renewal, a fresh start. What needs to change, what will take your forward, breathe new life into things? Keep moving forward, let in sunlight, allow the shoots to grow.

STORKS CARD COMBINATIONS

STORK & RIDER: NEW BEGINNING UPCOMING; THE ARRIVAL OF SOMEONE NEW

STORK & CLOVER: OPPORTUNITY FOR A FRESH START; LUCKY NEW BEGINNING

STORK & SHIP: FIRST LEG OF A TRIP;JOURNEY BEGINS; TRAVELLING AFRESH

STORK & HOUSE: HOUSE MOVE; FRESH START FOR THE FAMILY

STORK & TREE: NEW LEASE OF LIFE; RECOVERY; HEALTH IMPROVES

STORK & CLOUDS: RISKY NEW START; TAKE THINGS AS THEY COME; UNFOCUSED

STORK & SNAKE: PROBLEMATIC BEGINNING; TROUBLED START

STORK & COFFIN: FALSE START; CANCELLATION;

STORK & BOUQUET: HAPPY FRESH START; IMPROVEMENTS; POSITIVE CHANGES

STORK & SCYTHE: UNEXPECTED OR SUDDEN CHANGE

STORK & WHIP: TOUGH BEGINNING; DIFFICULT CHANGE

STORK & BIRDS: NEWS OF CHANGE; TALKING ABOUT FRESH START

STORK & CHILD: BIRTH; PREGNANCY; BEGINNER

STORK & FOX: CHANGE OF JOB; NEW START AT WORK

STORK & BEAR: FINANCIAL FRESH START; POWERFUL CHANGE

STORK & STARS: RISING STAR; HOPEFUL NEW BEGINNING; PROGRESS

STORK & DOG: NEW FRIENDSHIP; RENEWED LOYALTY

STORK & TOWER: CHANGES AT THE TOP; NEW GOVERNMENT

STORK & GARDEN: GROUP CHANGES OR BEGINS; PUBLIC CHANGE

STORK & MOUNTAIN: START DELAYED; OBSTACLES TO CHANGE

STORK & CROSSROAD: NEW PATHS AHEAD; FRESH OPTIONS

STORK & MICE: WORRYING CHANGES; FIRST DAY NERVES

STORK & HEART: NEW ROMANCE; RELATIONSHIP FRESH START

STORK & RING: HONEYMOON PERIOD; NEW CONTRACT; PROMISE

STORK & BOOK: LEARNING SOMETHING NEW; FRESH LEAD;

STORK & LETTER: NEWS OF CHANGE; SIGN-OFF RECEIVED

STORK & MAN: NEW START FOR A MAN; FLEXIBLE MAN; PROGRESSIVE

STORK & WOMAN: NEW START FOR A WOMAN; FLEXIBLE WOMAN; PROGRESSIVE

STORK & LILY: LATER LIFE CHANGES; MATURITY

STORK & SUN: SUCCESSFUL NEW START; SUCCESSFUL CHANGES

STORK & MOON: CREATIVE START; EMOTIONAL NEW BEGINNING; HAPPINESS

STORK & KEY: SIGNIFICANT START; IMPORTANT CHANGE; LIFE-CHANGING

STORK & FISH: EARLY-STAGE BUSINESS; BUSINESS CHANGE

STORK & ANCHOR: STABLE BEGINNING; LONG TERM PROGRESS

STORK & CROSS: DIFFICULT START; UNPLEASANT CHANGE; HARDER THAN ANTICIPATE

18. DOG

Playing Card	**Ten of Hearts**
General (Noun)	Friendship, Companion, Support, Ally, Loyalty, Advice
General (Adj)	Friendly, Supportive, Advisory, Loyal, Faithful, Reliable
Love	Companion, Faithfulness & Loyalty. Trust. Another Partner
Career	Colleagues, Advisors, Loyal Customers, Business Partners,
People	Helpers, Friends, Supporters. Mentors, Guides, Carers
Timing	Eighteen Days, Eighteenth Day of the Month

Card's Message

Old faithful. Who can you rely on at this time? Who are your friends, your support? Friendship and kindness wins the day. Advice and guidance is there when you need it.

Dog Card Combinations

DOG & RIDER:	VISIT FROM A FRIEND; SOMEONE NEW ARRIVES IN YOUR LIFE
DOG & CLOVER:	LUCKY FRIENDSHIP OR FRIEND; FRIEND BRINGS LUCK
DOG & SHIP:	OVERSEAS FRIEND; TRAVELLING COMPANION
DOG & HOUSE:	FAITHFUL PARTNER; FAMILY FRIEND; COMPANION
DOG & TREE:	KARMIC RETURN; FIT FRIEND; GROWING SUPPORT
DOG & CLOUDS:	DODGY FRIEND; CONFUSED FRIEND
DOG & SNAKE:	BETRAYAL FROM SOMEONE YOU TRUST; DISLOYALTY
DOG & COFFIN:	END OF A FRIENDSHIP; END-OF-LIFE SUPPORT
DOG & BOUQUET:	HAPPY FRIENDSHIP; GOOD-LOOKING FRIEND
DOG & SCYTHE:	ABANDONMENT; CUT-OFF FRIENDSHIP; DECISIVE FRIEND
DOG & WHIP:	FRIENDS-WITH-BENEFITS; HARSH FRIEND; TRAINER, COACH
DOG & BIRDS:	CHATTY FRIEND; TALKING WITH FRIENDS; FLATMATES
DOG & CHILD:	CHILDHOOD FRIEND; YOUNG FRIENDSHIP
DOG & FOX:	COLLEAGUE; SNEAKY FRIEND
DOG & BEAR:	WEALTHY FRIEND; FINANCIAL ADVISOR; BODYGUARD
DOG & STARS:	FAMOUS FRIEND; HIGH-FLIER YOU KNOW; BEST PAL
DOG & STORKS	FRESH START IN A FRIENDSHIP; START OF A NEW FRIENDSHIP
DOG & TOWER:	FRIENDS IN HIGH PLACES; OFFICIAL ADVISER; LAWYER

DOG & GARDEN:	GROUP OF FRIENDS; PARTY, CELEBRATION
DOG & MOUNTAIN:	BLOCKED FRIENDSHIP; HARD-GOING FRIENDSHIP
DOG & CROSSROAD:	LOTS OF FRIENDS; CHOICE OF FRIENDS; GUIDE OR MENTOR
DOG & MICE:	ANXIOUS FRIEND; STRESSFUL FRIENDSHIP
DOG & HEART:	GREAT FRIEND; SOULMATE; CLOSE BUDDY; LIFE PARTNER
DOG & RING:	PARTNER; MARRIED FRIEND; LIFE COMPANION; ALLY
DOG & BOOK:	SECRET FRIEND; CLASSMATE; FELLOW RESEARCHER
DOG & LETTER:	PENPAL; INTERNET FRIEND
DOG & MAN:	MALE FRIEND; MALE FRIENDSHIPS; MAN AND PARTNER
DOG & WOMAN:	FEMALE FRIEND; FEMALE FRIENDSHIPS; WOMAN AND
DOG & LILY:	OLD FRIEND; LIFELONG COMPANION
DOG & SUN:	POSITIVE FRIENDSHIP; SUCCESSFUL FRIEND
DOG & MOON:	EMOTIONAL FRIENDSHIP; CREATIVE COLLEAGUE
DOG & KEY:	SIGNIFICANT FRIEND; PAST LIFE RETURN
DOG & FISH:	BUSINESS ASSOCIATE; MENTOR; ADVISER
DOG & ANCHOR:	STABLE FRIENDSHIP; RELIABLE FRIEND
DOG & CROSS:	DIFFICULT OR CO-DEPENDENT FRIENDSHIP; COUNSELLING

19. TOWER

Playing Card	**Six of Spades**
General (Noun)	Officialdom, Government, Organisation, Building, Status
General (adj)	Official, Legal, Government, Structural, Established
Love:	Ego, Established Relationship, Making it Official, Legalities
Career:	Corporations, Officials, Legality, the Establishment.
People:	Well-Established, Egotistical, Authoritative, Status-Conscious
Timing:	Nineteen Days, Weeks, Nineteenth of the Month

Card's Message

Officialdom and status comes into play. What are the rules and regulations in the situation? Are they helpful - or stifling? Look at the structures around you. Ensure they're as solid as you need them to be

TOWER CARD COMBINATIONS

TOWER & RIDER: ARRIVAL OF AUTHORITIES; OFFICIAL VISIT; AUTHORITARIAN

TOWER & CLOVER: LUCKY ORGANIZATION; SUCCESSFUL COMPANY; CASINO

TOWER & SHIP: GLOBAL CORPORATION; VISA REQUIREMENTS; AIRPORT

TOWER & HOUSE: CASTLE; FLATS; ESTATE AGENTS; GOVT DEPARTMENT

TOWER & TREE: HEALTH CENTRE, HOSPITAL; DEPARTMENT OF HEALTH, N.H.S.

TOWER & CLOUDS: SHADY AUTHORITIES; PROPAGANDISTS; MAFIA

TOWER & SNAKE: UNTRUSTWORTHY ORGANIZATION; CORRUPTION;

TOWER & COFFIN: MAUSOLEUM, FUNERAL PARLOUR; FALL OF GOVERNMENT

TOWER & BOUQUET: BEAUTY OR FASHION INDUSTRY; BEAUTIFUL BUILDING

TOWER & SCYTHE: GOVERNMENT CUTS; LOSS OF STATURE; OFFICIAL DECISION

TOWER & WHIP: TOUGH OFFICIALS; PRISON; GYM; STRUGGLE FOR STATUS

TOWER & BIRDS: PARLIAMENT; OFFICIAL NEWS; LEGAL TALKS

TOWER & CHILD: CHILDREN'S ORGANIZATION; SCHOOL

TOWER & FOX :   CORPORATE WORK; OFFICIAL BUSINESS; LAWYER; OFFICIAL DECEIT

TOWER & BEAR: BANK; TAX OFFICE; TREASURY; POWERFUL ORGANISATION

TOWER & STARS: STAR STATUS; BIG EGO; PR MACHINE

TOWER & STORKS: GETTING ESTABLISHED; MAKING IT OFFICIAL; NEW GOVT

TOWER & DOG: ANIMAL SHELTER; OFFICIAL SUPPORT, FRIENDLY OFFICIAL

TOWER & GARDEN:	PUBLIC ORGANIZATION; PUBLIC BUILDING
TOWER & MOUNTAIN:	BLOCKED BY OFFICIALS; INSURMOUNTABLE DELAYS
TOWER & CROSSROAD	ORGANISATIONAL CHOICES; OFFICIAL DIRECTION
TOWER & MICE:	CRUMBLING STRUCTURE; CORPORATE WORRIES
TOWER & HEART:	DATING ORGANIZATION; CHARITABLE ORGANISATION
TOWER & RING:	GOVERNMENT CONTRACT; CORPORATE DEAL
TOWER & BOOK:	SCHOOL, COLLEGE, UNIVERSITY; BIG PUBLISHER
TOWER & LETTER:	POST OFFICE; NEWS ORGANIZATION; OFFICIAL NOTICE
TOWER & MAN:	MALE OFFICIAL; GURU FIGURE; EXPERT
TOWER & WOMAN:	FEMALE OFFICIAL; WOMAN'S STATUS; EXPERT
TOWER & LILY	OLD PEOPLE'S CHARITY; ESTABLISHED ORGANISATION
TOWER & SUN:	'MAKING IT'; SUCCESSFUL ORGANIZATION; HIGH STATUS
TOWER & MOON:	EMOTIONAL WITHDRAWAL; CREATIVE ORGANISATION
TOWER & KEY:	GOVERNMENT; SIGNIFICANT ORGANIZATION; MAJOR CORPORATION
TOWER & FISH:	BUSINESS REGISTRY; TRADE ORGANISATION
TOWER & ANCHOR:	LONG TERM STATUS; ESTABLISHMENT
TOWER & CROSS:	CHURCH; DIFFICULTY WITH AUTHORITIES

20. GARDEN

Playing Card	**Eight of Spades**
General (Noun)	Outdoors, Public, Group, Marketplace, World, Event, Garden
General (Adj)	Public, Open, Social, Group, Shared, Outdoor, Community
Love	Sociable, On the Market, Out There, Dating, Wedding, Parties
Career	Community Work, Marketing, Events, PR, Work With Public
People	Sociable, Gregarious, Extravert, Joiner, Public-Spirited
Timing	Twenty Days, Weeks, Twentieth of the Month

Card's Message

Get out there! Socialise, network, join groups, get involved in the community around you. Meet new people, reach out.

GARDEN CARD COMBINATIONS

GARDEN & RIDER: PARTY INVITE; A MORE SOCIABLE PERIOD; VISITORS

GARDEN & CLOVER: FORTUNATE GROUP; LUCKY EVENT

GARDEN & SHIP: TRAVEL COMPANIONS; TOUR PARTY

GARDEN & HOUSE: HOUSE PARTY; DOMESTIC GATHERING; LARGE FAMILY

GARDEN & TREE: KARMIC MEETING; PUBLIC HEALTH; SPA

GARDEN & CLOUDS: DIFFICULT CROWD; PROBLEMS IN A GROUP

GARDEN & SNAKE: SNAKE IN THE GRASS; BETRAYAL IN A GROUP

GARDEN & COFFIN: END OF SOCIABILITY; PARTY CANCELLATION; SOCIAL SHAME

GARDEN & BOUQUET: LOVELY GATHERING; PLEASANT MEETING; GARDEN PARTY

GARDEN & SCYTHE: PUBLIC DECISION OR WILL; OSTRACISM; RECLUSIVENESS

GARDEN & WHIP: UNFORGIVING PUBLIC; ARGUMENT; ORGY; TRAINING GROUP

GARDEN & BIRDS: PUBLIC SPEECH; DISCUSSION GROUP; SOCIAL MEDIA

GARDEN & CHILD: CLASS; SCHOOL-FRIENDS; PLAYGROUP; BEGINNER'S GROUP

GARDEN & FOX: WORK COLLEAGUES AND ASSOCIATES; NETWORK

GARDEN & BEAR: MARKETPLACE; PRIZE DRAW

GARDEN & STARS: GALA; AWARD CEREMONY; CONSTELLATION; FANS

GARDEN & STORKS: A NEW CROWD OR NETWORK; PUBLIC FRESH START

GARDEN & DOG: FRIENDSHIP GROUP; SUPPORTIVE NETWORK

GARDEN & TOWER:	ORGANISATIONS; PUBLIC BUILDING; LEADERSHIP
GARDEN & MOUNTAIN:	BLOCKED SOCIABILITY; CANCELLATION OF EVENT
GARDEN & CROSSROAD:	PUBLIC OPTIONS; CHOICE OF SOCIAL GROUPS
GARDEN & MICE:	ANXIOUS PUBLIC; WORRIED ASSOCIATES
GARDEN & HEART:	DATING POOL; PUBLIC ROMANTIC EVENT
GARDEN & RING:	MEMBERSHIP; WEDDING
GARDEN & BOOK:	COLLEGE; HIDDEN NETWORK; KNOWLEDGE SHARING
GARDEN & LETTER:	ANNOUNCEMENT; PUBLIC DOCUMENTS; INVITATION
GARDEN & MAN:	SOCIABLE MAN; MALE GROUP; MEN AS A WHOLE
GARDEN & WOMAN:	SOCIABLE WOMAN; FEMALE GROUP; WOMEN AS A WHOLE
GARDEN & LILY:	LONGSTANDING NETWORK; OLDER GROUP; MATURE GATHERING
GARDEN & SUN:	SUCCESSFUL SUPPORT NETWORK; PUBLIC SUCCESS
GARDEN & MOON:	AUDIENCE FOR CREATIVITY; PUBLIC; SUPPORT GROUP
GARDEN & KEY:	SIGNIFICANT NETWORK; PUBLIC IMPORTANCE
GARDEN & FISH:	BUSINESS ASSOCIATES; NETWORKING
GARDEN & ANCHOR:	STABLE ASSOCIATIONS; LONG-TERM GROUP
GARDEN & CROSS:	THERAPY GROUP; RELIGIOUS CONGREGATION

21.MOUNTAIN

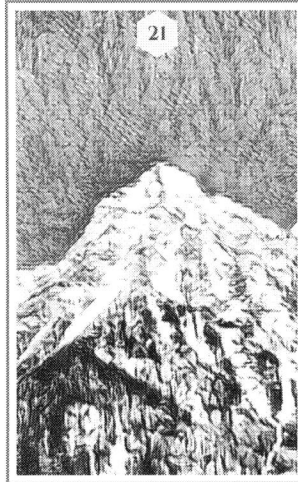

Playing Card	**Eight of Clubs**
General (Noun)	Block, Delay, Obstacle, Stop, Prevention, Isolation
General (Adj)	Delayed, Blocked, Stopped, Difficult, Isolated, Unyielding
Love	Unhappily Single, Rigidity. Obstacles or Blocks to Love.
Career	Challenges. Delays, Obstacles. Climber, Ski-ing.
People	Stubborn Individuals, Rigid, Immovable. Isolation.
Timing:	Three Months, Twenty-One days, Twenty-First. Winter

Card's Message

What is getting in the way? What obstacles need to be overcome? Remember, there are always ways around problems. Or do you need to stand your ground?

Mountain Card Combinations

MOUNTAIN & RIDER:	DELAYED ARRIVAL; LATE DELIVERY
MOUNTAIN & CLOVER:	EVENTUAL LUCK; THINGS IMPROVE
MOUNTAIN & SHIP:	JOURNEY DELAY; CANCELLED TRIP
MOUNTAIN & HOUSE:	ISOLATION; PROBLEMS WITH HOUSE SALE
MOUNTAIN & TREE:	HEALTH ISSUES; DELAYS IN RECOVERY
MOUNTAIN & CLOUDS:	CONFUSIONS AND BLOCKAGES; HIDDEN OBSTACLE
MOUNTAIN & SNAKE:	PROBLEMS AND DELAYS
MOUNTAIN & COFFIN:	FINALITY; END OF OBSTACLES
MOUNTAIN & BOUQUET:	MOUNTAIN RESORT; TAKING THE SCENIC ROUTE
MOUNTAIN & SCYTHE:	ACTION AFTER BLOCKAGE
MOUNTAIN & WHIP:	TOUGH TIMES; STRUGGLE
MOUNTAIN & BIRDS:	BLOCKED CONVERSATION; DELAYED MEETING
MOUNTAIN & CHILD:	SMALL OBSTACLE; ISOLATED CHILD; LATE STARTER
MOUNTAIN & FOX:	WORK DELAYS; BLOCKED CAREER
MOUNTAIN & BEAR:	FINANCIAL DELAYS; INCOME BLOCKED
MOUNTAIN & STARS:	CHALLENGING GOALS; ACHIEVEMENTS BLOCKED
MOUNTAIN & STORKS;	FRESH START DELAYED; FALSE START; ON THE MOVE AGAIN
MOUNTAIN & DOG:	BLOCKED FRIENDSHIP; ABANDONMENT

MOUNTAIN & TOWER:	OFFICIAL DELAYS; LEGAL RESTRICTION; PRISON
MOUNTAIN & GARDEN	GROUP BLOCKED, SLOWED DOWN
MOUNTAIN & CROSSROAD:	CHOICES BLOCKED; MULTIPLE DELAYS
MOUNTAIN & MICE:	ANXIETIES AND DELAYS; BETA BLOCKERS
MOUNTAIN & HEART:	LOVE BLOCKAGE; LONELY HEART
MOUNTAIN & RING:	RELATIONSHIP PREVENTED; CONTRACT DELAYS
MOUNTAIN & BOOK:	HIDDEN BLOCKAGE; KNOWLEDGE BLOCKED
MOUNTAIN & LETTER:	DELAYED MESSAGE
MOUNTAIN & MAN:	ISOLATED MAN; MAN CAUSES DELAYS
MOUNTAIN & WOMAN:	ISOLATED WOMAN; WOMAN CAUSES DELAYS
MOUNTAIN & LILY:	SLOWING DOWN IN OLD AGE; TAKING THINGS EASY
MOUNTAIN & SUN:	SUCCESS AFTER DELAY; SOMETHING SUCCESSFULLY PREVENTED
MOUNTAIN & MOON:	CREATIVE BLOCKAGE; PENT-UP EMOTIONS
MOUNTAIN & KEY:	SIGNIFICANT DELAY; BLOCKS OVERCOME
MOUNTAIN & FISH:	BUSINESS DELAY; FREEDOM PREVENTED; BUSINESS BLOCK
MOUNTAIN & ANCHOR:	STAGNANT; LONG-TERM BLOCKAGE; PERMANENT STOP
MOUNTAIN & CROSS:	DEPRESSION; INSURMOUNTABLE TROUBLE

22. CROSSROADS

Playing Card	**Queen of Diamonds**
General (noun)	Choices, Options, Paths, Fork, Crossroad
General (adj).	Several, Multiple, Many, Choice-Related, Picked
Love:	Non-Committal, Several Lovers, Multiple Dating, Choice
Career:	Career Paths or Directions, Several Jobs, Multiple Offers
People:	Indecisive, At a Crossroads, Lacking Commitment
Timing:	Twenty-Two Days, Weeks, Twenty-Second of the Month

Card's Message

A crossroads in life and there are multiple options ahead. Now is the time to make a choice, or decide which way you're going. Which is the right path for you?

CROSSROADS CARD COMBINATIONS

CROSSROAD & RIDER: ARRIVAL OF OPTIONS; CHOICE TO BE MADE; MESSAGES

CROSSROAD & CLOVER: FORTUNATE PATH; LUCKY CHOICES; POSITIVE WAYS AHEAD

CROSSROAD & SHIP: JOURNEY OPTIONS; CHOICE OF DIRECTION; ROUTE OR MAP

CROSSROAD & HOUSE: CHOICE OF HOME; FAMILY OPTIONS; DOMESTIC CHOICES

CROSSROAD & TREE: HEALTH OPTIONS OR OUTCOMES; KARMIC PATH; SPIRITUAL CHOICE

CROSSROAD & CLOUDS: THE WAY FORWARD UNCLEAR; UNCERTAINTY; CAN'T SEE AHEAD

CROSSROAD & SNAKE: A WRONG TURNING; DIFFICULT CHOICES; NO POSITIVE OPTIONS

CROSSROAD & COFFIN: THE END OF THE ROAD; NO CHOICE; FINAL OPTIONS

CROSSROAD & BOUQUET: PLEASANT CHOICES; HAPPY OUTCOME; POSITIVE ROADS AHEAD

CROSSROAD & SCYTHE: DECISIVENESS; ROAD ACCIDENT; REDUCED OPTIONS

CROSSROAD & WHIP: TOUGH CHOICES; FORCED OPTIONS; LIMITED ROADS AHEAD

CROSSROAD & BIRDS: PHONE LINE; NETWORK; COMMUNICATION OPTIONS

CROSSROAD & CHILD: CHILD'S CHOICES; EARLY OPTIONS; SIBLINGS; CHILD'S FUTURE

CROSSROAD & FOX: CAREER CROSSROADS; JOB OPTIONS; DECEPTIVE PATH

CROSSROAD & BEAR: FINANCIAL OPTIONS; SEVERAL INCOME STREAMS

CROSSROAD & STARS: PATH TO ACHIEVEMENT; GOAL-MAKING; AMBITIOUS ROAD AHEAD

CROSSROAD & STORKS: NEW DIRECTION; PROGRESS; NEW ROADS OPENING UP

CROSSROAD & DOG: CHOICE OF COMPANION; FRIENDSHIP PATH; HELPFUL GUIDANCE

CROSSROAD & TOWER: OFFICIAL PATHWAYS; LEGAL OPTIONS; GOVERNMENT CHOICES

CROSSROAD & GARDEN: SOCIABILITY; PARTIES; CHOICE OF EVENTS

CROSSROAD & MOUNTAIN ANALYSIS PARALYSIS; ALL AVENUES BLOCKED

CROSSROAD & MICE: OVERWHELM, TOO MANY OPTIONS; STRESS

CROSSROAD & HEART: SEVERAL LOVE INTERESTS; DATING OPTIONS; ROMANTIC CHOICES

CROSSROAD & RING: RELATIONSHIP CHOICE; CONTRACT OFFERS

CROSSROAD & BOOK: SECRET PATHWAY; LEARNING OPTIONS; DISCOVERY;

CROSSROAD & LETTER: MESSAGES SENT OUT; MAILING OPTIONS; NEWSLETTERS

CROSSROAD & MAN: MAN'S DECISIONS; NON-COMMITTAL

CROSSROAD & WOMAN: WOMAN'S DECISIONS; NON-COMMITTAL

CROSSROAD & LILY: MATURE CHOICES; PEACEFUL PATH

CROSSROAD & SUN: SUCCESSFUL ROUTE; RIGHT CHOICE

CROSSROAD & MOON: CREATIVE OPTIONS; EMOTIONAL CROSSROADS

CROSSROAD & KEY: SIGNIFICANT CHOICES; KEY TURNING POINT

CROSSROAD & FISH: MULTIPLE BUSINESSES; BUSINESS OPTIONS

CROSSROAD & ANCHOR: STABLE CHOICES; LONG TERM ROAD AHEAD

CROSSROAD & CROSS: TOUGH ROAD AHEAD; NO EASY CHOICE

23. MICE

Playing Card	**Seven of Clubs**
General (Noun)	Worry, Anxiety, Nerves, Infestation, Agitation, Apprehension
General (Adj)	Anxious, Nervy, Worried, Worrying, Gnawing, Niggling
Love	Clinginess, Neuroticism, Obsessive Behaviour. Love Worries.
Career:	Work Stress, Rat-Race, Pointless-Seeming Work, Wastefulness
People:	Anxious, Jittery, Neurotic, Unstable, Stressy, Highly-strung
Timing:	Twenty-Three Days, Twenty-Third, Very Soon, Rapidly

Card's Message

Anxiety, a stressful situation or worries around. Are you letting small problems get to you, making mountains out of molehills? Or is there a small problem you're ignoring but that's niggling at you? Deal with it before it gets bigger.

Mice Card Combinations

MICE & RIDER:	TROUBLES AFOOT; VISITOR ANXIETY; WORRYING
MICE & CLOVER:	BUTTERFLIES; ANXIOUS ANTICIPATION; TRUST YOUR GUT
MICE & SHIP:	FEAR OF FLYING; ANXIOUS TRIP; PROBLEMS ON A JOURNEY
MICE & HOUSE:	DOMESTIC NIGGLES; HOUSE WORRIES; FAMILY ISSUES
MICE & TREE:	HEALTH CONCERNS; SYMPTOMS OF ANXIETY
MICE & CLOUDS:	LACK OF CLARITY CAUSES ANXIETY; DISTRESS; CONFUSION
MICE & SNAKE:	MAJOR PROBLEMS; PARANOIA
MICE & COFFIN:	WORRIES END; ANXIETY ABOUT AN ENDING; MORBIDITY
MICE & BOUQUET:	ANTICIPATION; NERVOUS EXCITEMENT; THRILL
MICE & SCYTHE:	ANXIETY ABOUT A DECISION; BREAKUP WORRIES
MICE & WHIP	STRESS AND PRESSURE; ARGUMENTS CAUSE ANXIETY
MICE & BIRDS	FEAR OF COMMUNICATION; WORRIED ABOUT A MEETING;
MICE & CHILD:	WORRIED ABOUT A CHILD; SMALL PROBLEMS
MICE & FOX:	JOB WORRIES; CAREER ANXIETY; WORK STRESS
MICE & BEAR:	MONEY WORRIES; FINANCIAL STRESS
MICE & STARS:	PERFORMANCE ANXIETY; PRESSURE
MICE & STORKS:	ANXIOUS ABOUT CHANGE; UNWANTED NEW START
MICE & DOG:	FRIENDSHIP WORRIES; ANXIOUS FRIEND

MICE & TOWER: OFFICIAL CONCERNS; LEGAL WORRIES

MICE & GARDEN: SOCIAL ANXIETY; AGORAPHOBIA

MICE & MOUNTAIN: DELAYED ANXIETY; LONG TERM STRESS; PTSD

MICE & CROSSROAD: OPTION OVERLOAD; ANXIOUS OVER WHAT TO DO NEXT

MICE & HEART: LOVE WORRIES; ROMANTIC PROBLEMS; RELATIONSHIP STRESS

MICE & RING: CONTRACT DIFFICULTIES; MARRIAGE TROUBLES

MICE & BOOK: SECRET WORRIES;; STUDY STRESS

MICE & LETTER: TROUBLING NEWS; DOCUMENTED CONCERNS

MICE & MAN: MAN'S WORRIES; STRESSED MAN

MICE & WOMAN: WOMAN'S WORRIES; STRESSED WOMAN

MICE & LILY: AGEING WORRIES; DEMENTIA

MICE & SUN: ANXIOUS ABOUT SUCCESS; EVENTUAL VICTORY

MICE & MOON: EMOTIONAL TROUBLES; CREATIVE CONCERNS

MICE & KEY: SIGNIFICANT CONCERN; IMPORTANT WORRIES

MICE & FISH: BUSINESS PROBLEMS; FREELANCER WORRIES

MICE & ANCHOR: LONG-TERM ANXIETY; CONSTANT STATE OF WORRY

MICE & CROSS   TROUBLED; BURDENED; MAJOR ANXIETY

24. HEART

Playing Card	**Jack of Hearts**
General (noun)	Love, Love-Life, Romance, Passion, Warmth, Desire, Care
General (Adj)	Loving, Romantic, Heartfelt, Passionate, Desired, Caring
Love:	Romance, Love Life, a Love or Lover, Passionate Feelings
Career:	Passion, Caring work, Vocation, Office Romance, Matchmaking
People:	Loving, Caring, Warm, Passionate, Heart-Over-Head, Romantic
Timing:	Twenty-Four Days, Twenty-Fourth, Summer

Card's Message

Love is in the air! A romance or passionate enterprise, your heart's desire, humanitarian issues. Be loving and warm, follow your passion.

Heart Card Combinations

Heart & Rider: NEW LOVER; ARRIVAL OF ROMANCE

Heart & Clover: LUCKY ROMANCE; HAPPY LOVE LIFE

Heart & Ship: ROMANTIC TRIP; HOLIDAY ROMANCE

Heart & House: HEARTH & HOME; DOMESTIC BLISS; LOVING FAMILY

Heart & Tree: HEALTHY HEART; KARMIC LOVE; GROWING ROMANCE

Heart & Clouds: CONFUSING ROMANCE; UNCLEAR ROMANTIC INTENTIONS

Heart & Snake: ROMANTIC BETRAYAL; CHEATING HEART

Heart & Coffin: END OF A ROMANCE; BROKEN HEART

Heart & Bouquet: BLOSSOMING LOVE; ROMANTIC HAPPINESS; WEDDING

Heart & Scythe: HEARTBROKEN; DAMAGED HEART; HEART SURGERY

Heart & Whip: SEXUAL DESIRE; TOUGH LOVE; CHALLENGING ROMANCE;

Heart & Birds: SWEET-TALK; ROMANTIC CONVERSATION; LOVEBIRDS

Heart & Child: CHILD'S LOVE; CHILDLIKE LOVE; YOUNG LOVE

Heart & Fox: STOLEN HEART; CAREER PASSIONS; PLAYER; DECEPTIVE LOVE

Heart & Bear   PROTECTIVE LOVE; FINANCIAL PROVIDER; POWERFUL LOVE

Heart & Stars: CELEBRITY CRUSH; IDEALISTIC LOVE

Heart & Storks: NEW ROMANCE BEGINNING; STARTING TO DATE AGAIN

Heart & Dog: FAITHFUL LOVE; SOULMATE; FIDELITY

HEART & TOWER:	MAKING IT OFFICIAL; HIGH-STATUS ROMANCE; CORE VALUES
HEART & GARDEN:	WEDDING; GOING PUBLIC WITH ROMANCE; FANDOM
HEART & MOUNTAIN:	BLOCKED ROMANCE; HARD-HEARTED; LONELY HEART
HEART & CROSSROAD:	ROMANTIC OPTIONS; CHOICE OF PASSIONS
HEART & MICE:	ROMANTIC ANXIETIES; ANXIOUS, CLINGY ROMANCE
HEART & RING:	MARRIAGE; ENGAGEMENT; MARRIED LOVE
HEART & BOOK:	SECRET ROMANCE; AFFAIR; ACADEMIC PASSION
HEART & LETTER:	LOVE LETTER; ROMANTIC MESSAGE; LOVE POEM
HEART & MAN:	MALE LOVER; PARTNER; MAN'S LOVE
HEART & WOMAN:	FEMALE LOVER; PARTNER; WOMAN'S LOVE
HEART & LILY:	ENDURING LOVE; LATER-LIFE ROMANCE; WISE HEART
HEART & SUN:	HAPPY ROMANCE; JOYFUL LOVE
HEART & MOON:	ROMANTIC LOVE; EMOTIVE ROMANCE; CREATIVE PASSION
HEART & KEY:	SIGNIFICANT LOVE; THE ONE; DESTINED; SOULMATE
HEART & FISH:	FREE AGENT; NO-STRINGS AFFAIR; BUSINESS PASSION
HEART & ANCHOR:	LONG-LASTING LOVE; LONG-TERM ROMANCE
HEART & CROSS:	TROUBLED ROMANCE; CODEPENDENCY; HEAVY HEART

25. RING

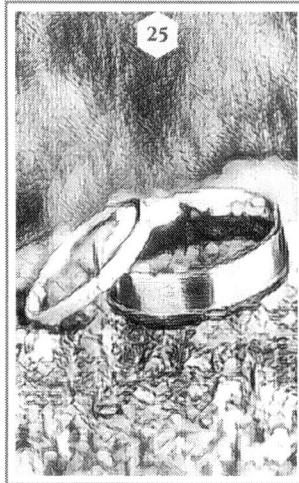

Playing Card	Ace of Clubs
General (Noun)	Relationship, Agreement, Marriage, Contract, Bond, Promise
General (Adj)	Agreed, Married, Taken, Contracted, Promised, Committed
Love	Marriage, Already Taken, Commitment, Engagement, Proposal
Career	Deal, Contract, Agreement, Bond or Payment. Partnerships.
People	Married, Committed, True to Their Word
Timing:	Continual, Repeated, Twenty-Five days, Twenty-Fifth

Card's Message

Stick to your promises. Do what you say you will, fulfil your agreements or contracts, be true to your word. What agreements have you entered into? Fulfil your side of the bargain

Ring Card Combinations

RING & RIDER:	CONTRACT ON THE WAY; NEW DEAL; PROPOSAL
RING & CLOVER:	FORTUNATE CONTRACT; LUCKY DEAL; HAPPY MARRIAGE
RING & SHIP:	OVERSEAS CONTRACT; TRAVEL BOOKING
RING & HOUSE:	RENTAL AGREEMENT; HOUSE SALE; FAMILY RELATIONSHIPS
RING & TREE:	KARMIC RETURN; BUDDING RELATIONSHIP; SPIRITUAL LINK
RING & CLOUDS:	BAD CONTRACT; UNCLEAR TERMS; CONFUSING RELATIONSHIP
RING & SNAKE:	UNTRUSTWORTHY CONTRACT; BETRAYED MARRIAGE
RING & COFFIN:	END OF A CONTRACT; RELATIONSHIP OVER
RING & BOUQUET:	WEDDING; HAPPY RELATIONSHIP; AGREEABLE CONTRACT
RING & SCYTHE:	BREAK-UP; CUT TIES; BROKEN CONTRACT
RING & WHIP:	TOUGH TERMS; ARGUMENTATIVE OR ABUSIVE RELATIONSHIP
RING & BIRDS:	NEGOTIATION; RELATIONSHIP DISCUSSION;
RING & CHILD:	ADOPTION; PARENTAL BOND; CHILD'S RELATIONSHIP
RING & FOX:	WORK AGREEMENT; WILY CONTRACT
RING & BEAR:	PAYMENT; FINANCIAL CONTRACT; POWERFUL RELATIONSHIP
RING & STARS:	CELEB MARRIAGE; HIGH PROFILE CONTRACT; STICK TO GOALS
RING & STORKS:	FRESH MARRIAGE OR RELATIONSHIP; NEW CONTRACT
RING & DOG:	FRIENDLY AGREEMENT; STRONG FRIENDSHIP

RING & TOWER: OFFICIAL AGREEMENT, SIGNED CONTRACT; LEGAL TERMS

RING & GARDEN: GROUP MEMBERSHIP; PUBLIC AGREEMENT; WEDDING PARTY

RING & MOUNTAIN: OBSTACLES TO AGREEMENT; DELAYED MARRIAGE

RING & CROSSROAD: BIGAMY; AGREEMENT OPTIONS; CHOICE OF CONTRACTS

RING & MICE: ANXIOUS RELATIONSHIP; UNHAPPILY MARRIED

RING & HEART: ROMANTIC COMMITMENT, MARRIAGE; LOVE PARTNERSHIP

RING & BOOK: SECRET AGREEMENT; HIDDEN TERMS; BOOK DEAL

RING & LETTER: WRITTEN AGREEMENT; CERTIFICATE; WEDDING INVITE

RING & MAN: HUSBAND; MAN'S MARRIAGE; MAN'S WORD

RING & WOMAN: WIFE, WOMAN'S MARRIAGE; WOMAN'S WORD

RING & LILY: MATURE AGREEMENT; OLDER MARRIAGE

RING & SUN: SUCCESSFUL RELATIONSHIP; HAPPY MARRIAGE; GOOD DEAL

RING & MOON: EMOTIONAL RELATIONSHIP; CREATIVE AGREEMENT

RING & KEY: KEY RELATIONSHIP; DESTINY, KARMA; IMPORTANT CONTRACT

RING & FISH: BUSINESS DEAL; PAYMENT

RING & ANCHOR: STABLE RELATIONSHIP; MARRIAGE; SECURITY; LASTING AGREEMENT

RING & CROSS   WEIGHED-DOWN RELATIONSHIP; OPPRESSIVE DEAL

26. BOOK

Playing Card	**Ten of Diamonds**
General (Noun)	Education, Learning, Knowledge, Secret, Books, Research
General (Adj)	Educational, Hidden, Secret, Knowledgeable, Learning,
Love	Secret, Clandestine, Wisdom, Romantic Knowledge
Career	Manual, Knowledge, Educational, College, School, Library
People	Learned, Knowledgeable, Well-Educated, Lecturers, Researchers
Timing	Unknown, Hidden; Twenty Six Days, Twenty-Sixth

.Card's Message

What is there to learn or know? What is hidden or yet to be discovered? Keep the mystery- or alternatively, keep digging. Never lose your curiosity or desire to learn.

26. BOOK

BOOK & RIDER: KNOWLEDGE OR INFORMATION ARRIVES

BOOK & CLOVER: LUCKY KNOWLEDGE; FORTUNATE SECRET; GREAT DISCOVERY

BOOK & SHIP: EXPLORATION; FOREIGN LEARNING; TRAVEL GUIDE

BOOK & HOUSE: FAMILY SECRET; D.I.Y. MANUAL; FAMILY KNOWLEDGE

BOOK & TREE: SPIRITUAL KNOWLEDGE; HEALTH SECRET; HIDDEN ILLNESS

BOOK & CLOUDS: MISINTERPRETATION; OBSCURED KNOWLEDGE; INCORRECT

BOOK & SNAKE: FALSE INFORMATION; BETRAYED SECRET

BOOK & COFFIN: LEARNING ENDS; SECRET UNCOVERED

BOOK & BOUQUET: PLEASANT DISCOVERY; BEAUTY SECRETS; LEARNING

BOOK & SCYTHE: SUDDEN REVEAL; HURTFUL SECRET; RAPID LEARNING

BOOK & WHIP: SEX SECRET; HIDDEN ABUSE; TOUGH SCHOOLING

BOOK & BIRDS: GOSSIP; STORYTELLING; LECTURE, CLASS; AUDIO-BOOK

BOOK & CHILD   SCHOOLWORK; BEGINNER'S MANUAL; CHILD'S SECRET

BOOK & FOX: WORK SECRET; JOB KNOWLEDGE; ACADEMIC AUTHOR

BOOK & BEAR   FINANCIAL KNOWLEDGE; POWERFUL SECRET; ACCOUNTS

BOOK & STARS   CELEB SECRET, TOP EDUCATION; BESTSELLER

BOOK & STORKS: BRAND-NEW KNOWLEDGE; LATEST DISCOVERY; FRESH SECRET

BOOK & DOG: FRIEND'S SECRET; SUPPORTING KNOWLEDGE; ADVICE

BOOK & TOWER: OFFICIAL SECRET; LEGAL KNOWLEDGE; ACADEMIA; RULES

BOOK & GARDEN: PUBLIC KNOWLEDGE; CLASS; PUBLIC EDUCATION; LESSON

BOOK & MOUNTAIN: BLOCKED EDUCATION; OBSTACLES TO DISCOVERY

BOOK & CROSSROAD: MULTIPLE SOURCES OF INFO; MANY SECRETS

BOOK & MICE   STRESSFUL SECRET; LEARNING ANXIETY; WORRYING INFORMATION

BOOK & HEART: SECRET CRUSH; ROMANTIC SECRET; LOVE WISDOM

BOOK & RING: MARRIAGE SECRETS; CONTRACT LAW; AGREEMENT INFORMATION

BOOK & LETTER: MANUAL; NEWSPAPER; NEWS OF A SECRET; PUBLISHING

BOOK & MAN: MAN'S KNOWLEDGE; MALE AUTHOR; MALE ACADEMIC

BOOK & WOMAN: WOMAN'S KNOWLEDGE; FEMALE AUTHOR; FEMALE ACADEMIC

BOOK & LILY: LONGSTANDING SECRET; WISDOM, LIFE EXPERIENCE

BOOK & SUN: SECRET REVEALED; ACADEMIC SUCCESS; SUCCESSFUL BOOK

BOOK & MOON: EMOTIONAL SECRET; NOVEL; INSTINCTIVE KNOWLEDGE

BOOK & KEY: IMPORTANT SECRET; KEY INFORMATION; SIGNIFICANT KNOWLEDGE

BOOK & FISH: BUSINESS LEARNING; BUSINESS SECRET; FREELANCE KNOWLEDGE

BOOK & ANCHOR: ESTABLISHED KNOWLEDGE; NEVER-REVEALED SECRET

BOOK & CROSS: TROUBLING SECRET; WEIGHTY SECRET; DIFFICULT KNOWLEDGE

27. LETTER

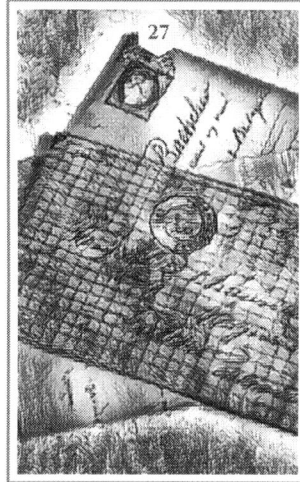

Playing Card	**Seven of Spades**
General (Noun)	Letter, Message, Document, Paperwork, Writing, News, Post
General (Adj)	Written, Documented, Reported, Signed, Recorded, Certified
Love:	Love Letters, Messaging, Texting, Poetry, Invitation
Career:	Documents, Contracts, Signatures, Paper Trail, Writer
People:	Authors, Journalists, Bloggers, Penpals, Posters Online
Timing	Twenty-Seven Days, Twenty-Seventh of the Month

Card's Message

The arrival of messages, mail, announcements or news. Check your paperwork, get it in writing.

LETTER CARD COMBINATIONS

LETTER & RIDER: NEWS ARRIVES, MESSAGE DELIVERY

LETTER & CLOVER: FORTUNATE NEWS; LUCKY MESSAGE; WINNING TICKET

LETTER & SHIP: NEWS FROM OVERSEAS; LETTER IN TRANSIT

LETTER & HOUSE: DEEDS FOR A HOUSE; HOME DOCUMENTS; FAMILY NEWS

LETTER & TREE: HEALTH LETTER; HEALTH CERTIFICATE; SPIRITUAL MESSAGE

LETTER & CLOUDS: UNCLEAR DOCUMENTATION; CONFUSING NEWS

LETTER & SNAKE: BAD NEWS; NEWS OF A BETRAYAL

LETTER & COFFIN: FINAL LETTER; BEREAVEMENT NEWS; NEWS OF AN ENDING

LETTER & BOUQUET: LOVELY MESSAGE; INVITATION; POSITIVE NEWS

LETTER & SCYTHE: HURTFUL MESSAGE; NEWS OF DECISION; REDUNDANCY NEWS

LETTER & WHIP: DIFFICULT NEWS; ABUSIVE MESSAGE; HARSH FEEDBACK

LETTER & BIRDS: SOCIAL MEDIA MESSAGE; TEXT; CONVERSATIONAL LETTER

LETTER & CHILD: CHILD'S MESSAGE; NEWS OF A CHILD; PREGNANCY NEWS

LETTER & FOX: WORK DOCUMENTS; EMPLOYEE NEWS; DECEPTIVE MESSAGE

LETTER & BEAR: FINANCIAL DOCUMENTS; FORCEFUL LETTER; MONEY NEWS

LETTER & STARS: CELEBRITY PRESS; ACHIEVEMENT CERTIFICATE

LETTER & STORKS: NEWS OF CHANGE; NEW START DOCUMENTATION

LETTER & DOG   FRIEND'S LETTER; NEWS OF FRIEND; WRITTEN SUPPORT

LETTER & TOWER: OFFICIAL DOCUMENTS; PAPERS; CORPORATE NEWS

LETTER & GARDEN: PUBLIC ANNOUNCEMENT; EVENT INVITATION

LETTER & MOUNTAIN: DELAYED MESSAGE; NEWS BLOCKED; UNDELIVERED LETTER

LETTER & CROSSROAD: MAILINGS; MULTI-PLATFORM INFO; MANY DOCUMENTS

LETTER & MICE: WORRYING NEWS; ANXIOUS MESSAGE

LETTER & HEART: LOVE LETTER; ROMANTIC MESSAGE; NEWS OF A ROMANCE

LETTER & RING: CONTRACT; MARRIAGE CERTIFICATE; WRITTEN AGREEMENT

LETTER & BOOK: EXAM CERTIFICATE; HIDDEN MESSAGE; ESSAY

LETTER & MAN: MAN'S NEWS; MALE WRITER; MESSAGE FROM A MAN

LETTER & WOMAN: WOMAN'S NEWS; FEMALE WRITER; MESSAGE FROM A WOMAN

LETTER & LILY: MESSAGE FROM AN OLDER PERSON; WISE MESSAGE

LETTER & SUN: NEWS OF SUCCESS; HAPPY NEWS; POSITIVE MESSAGE

LETTER & MOON: CREATIVE WRITING; EMOTIONAL MESSAGE; POETRY

LETTER & KEY: IMPORTANT MESSAGE; SIGNIFICANT NEWS

LETTER & FISH: BUSINESS LETTER; BUSINESS EMAILS; BLOG

LETTER & ANCHOR: LONG-TERM NEWS; AGREEMENT; SAVED DOCUMENTS

LETTER & CROSS: DIFFICULT NEWS; PAINFUL MESSAGE; DEPRESSING NEWS

28. MAN

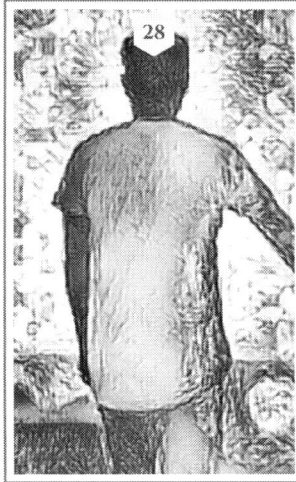

Playing Card	Ace of Hearts
General (Noun)	Man, Men, Males, The Querent
General (Adj)	Male, Man's, Mens', Masculine
Love	Querent/Man in Their Life. Men in general.
Career:	Querent/Man at Work. Male-Dominated Workplace
People:	Men, Males, Masculine
Timing:	Twenty-Eight Days or the Twenty-Eighth of the Month

Card's Message

You, if you are male, or a man in your life. Masculine energy.

MAN CARD COMBINATIONS

MAN & RIDER: MALE VISITOR; A NEW LOVER ON THE SCENE

MAN & CLOVER: LUCKY MAN; OPPORTUNISTIC INDIVIDUAL

MAN & SHIP: TRAVELLER; FOREIGN MAN

MAN & HOUSE: FAMILY MAN; LANDLORD

MAN & TREE: HEALTHY MAN; SPIRITUAL INDIVIDUAL; SHAMAN

MAN & CLOUDS: CONFUSED INDIVIDUAL; MISLEADING INDIVIDUAL

MAN & SNAKE   UNTRUSTWORTHY MAN; MAN BRINGS PROBLEMS

MAN & COFFIN   DEPRESSED MAN

MAN & BOUQUET: HANDSOME MAN; CHARMING INDIVIDUAL; PLEASANT MAN

MAN & SCYTHE: DECISIVE MAN; VIOLENT INDIVIDUAL ; ABRUPT PERSON

MAN & WHIP: ABUSIVE MAN; SPORTSMAN; TRAINER; SEXUAL MAN

MAN & BIRDS: TALKATIVE MAN; PRESS OFFICER; THERAPIST

MAN & CHILD: CHILDISH MAN; BOY; IMMATURE INDIVIDUAL

MAN & FOX: EMPLOYEE; CUNNING MAN; WHEELER-DEALER

MAN & BEAR: PROTECTIVE MAN; MALE MANAGER; PROVIDER

MAN & STARS: MALE CELEBRITY; HIGH-FLIER; ALPHA MALE; ASTRONAUT

MAN & STORKS: PROGRESSIVE MAN; FLEXIBLE INDIVIDUAL

MAN & DOG: MALE PARTNER; FRIENDLY MAN; MALE FRIEND

MAN & TOWER:	OFFICIAL; MALE LAWYER; TALL MAN; ARROGANT MAN
MAN & GARDEN:	SOCIABLE MAN; PUBLIC FIGURE; GROUP OF MEN
MAN & MOUNTAIN:	LONELY MAN; STUBBORN INDIVIDUAL; STICK-IN-THE-MUD
MAN & CROSSROAD:	COMMITMENT-PHOBE; MAN WITH CHOICES; SEVERAL MEN
MAN & MICE:	ANXIOUS MAN; STRESSED INDIVIDUAL
MAN & HEART:	LOVING MAN; LOVER; SOULMATE
MAN & RING:	HUSBAND; COMMITTED MAN; MARRIED MAN; LAWYER
MAN & BOOK:	AUTHOR; ACADEMIC; INTELLIGENT MAN; TEACHER
MAN & LETTER	WRITER; JOURNALIST; POSTMAN; BLOGGER
MAN & WOMAN:	COUPLE; MAN AND WOMAN
MAN & LILY:	FATHER; OLDER MAN; FATHER FIGURE; MENTOR
MAN & SUN:	SUCCESSFUL MAN; VICTOR; POSITIVE OR HAPPY MAN
MAN & MOON:	EMOTIONAL MAN; CREATIVE MAN
MAN & KEY:	SIGNIFICANT INDIVIDUAL; SOULMATE; IMPORTANT MAN
MAN & FISH:	BUSINESSMAN; FREELANCER; ENTREPRENEUR
MAN & ANCHOR:	SETTLED MAN; STABLE INDIVIDUAL; RELIABLE
MAN & CROSS	DEPRESSED MAN; PRIEST; SAINT

29. WOMAN

Playing Card	**Ace of Spades**
General (noun):	Woman, Female, Women, The Querent
General (adj):	Woman's, Female, Women's, Feminine
Love:	Querent / Woman In Their Life. Femininity, Female Energy.
Career:	Querent / Woman In Their Work Life. Female Industry
People:	Women, Female, Women in General.
Timing:	Twenty-Nine days or the Twenty-Ninth of the month.

Card's Message

You, if you are female, or a woman in your life. Feminine energy.

WOMAN CARD COMBINATIONS

WOMAN & RIDER: FEMALE VISITOR; A NEW FEMALE LOVER

WOMAN & CLOVER: LUCKY WOMAN; OPPORTUNISTIC INDIVIDUAL

WOMAN & SHIP: TRAVELLER; FOREIGN WOMAN

WOMAN & HOUSE: FAMILY WOMAN; HOUSEKEEPER; HOMEMAKER; LANDLADY

WOMAN & TREE: HEALTHY WOMAN; SPIRITUAL PERSON; HEALER

WOMAN & CLOUDS: CONFUSED WOMAN; MISLEADING INDIVIDUAL

WOMAN & SNAKE: UNTRUSTWORTHY WOMAN; TEMPTRESS

WOMAN & COFFIN: DEPRESSED WOMAN

WOMAN & BOUQUET: ATTRACTIVE WOMAN; CHARMING; NICE LADY

WOMAN & SCYTHE: DECISIVE WOMAN; HARSH INDIVIDUAL ; ABRUPT PERSON

WOMAN & WHIP: TOUGH WOMAN; SPORTSWOMAN; TRAINER; DOMINATRIX

WOMAN & BIRDS: CHATTY WOMAN; COMMUNICATOR; PRESS OFFICER;

WOMAN & CHILD: CHILDISH WOMAN; GIRL; IMMATURE INDIVIDUAL

WOMAN & FOX: EMPLOYEE; DECEITFUL WOMAN

WOMAN & BEAR: PROTECTIVE WOMAN; BOSS; MOTHER; WEALTHY WOMAN

WOMAN & STARS: FEMALE CELEB; HIGH-ACHIEVER; ALPHA FEMALE; ASTRONAUT

WOMAN & STORKS: PROGRESSIVE WOMAN; FLEXIBLE INDIVIDUAL

WOMAN & DOG: FEMALE PARTNER; FRIENDLY WOMAN; FEMALE FRIEND

WOMAN & TOWER:	OFFICIAL; FEMALE LAWYER; TALL WOMAN; QUEEN
WOMAN & GARDEN:	SOCIABLE WOMAN; PUBLIC FIGURE; GROUP OF WOMEN
WOMAN & MOUNTAIN:	LONELY WOMAN; STUBBORN INDIVIDUAL
WOMAN & CROSSROAD:	COMMITMENT-PHOBE; SEVERAL WOMEN; CHOOSY WOMAN
WOMAN & MICE:	ANXIOUS WOMAN; STRESSED INDIVIDUAL
WOMAN & HEART:	LOVING WOMAN; LOVER; SOULMATE
WOMAN & RING:	WIFE; COMMITTED WOMAN; MARRIED WOMAN
WOMAN & BOOK:	AUTHOR; ACADEMIC; INTELLIGENT WOMAN; TEACHER
WOMAN & LETTER:	WRITER; JOURNALIST; POSTWOMAN; BLOGGER
WOMAN & MAN:	COUPLE; WOMAN AND MAN
WOMAN & LILY:	OLDER WOMAN; GRANDMOTHER; MENTOR
WOMAN & SUN:	SUCCESSFUL WOMAN; WINNER; POSITIVE OR HAPPY WOMAN
WOMAN & MOON:	EMOTIONAL WOMAN; CREATIVE WOMAN
WOMAN & KEY:	SIGNIFICANT INDIVIDUAL; SOULMATE; IMPORTANT WOMAN
WOMAN & FISH:	BUSINESSWOMAN; FREELANCER; ENTREPRENEUR
WOMAN & ANCHOR:	SETTLED WOMAN; STABLE INDIVIDUAL; RELIABLE
WOMAN & CROSS:	DEPRESSED WOMAN; RELIGIOUS WOMAN; SAINT

30. LILY

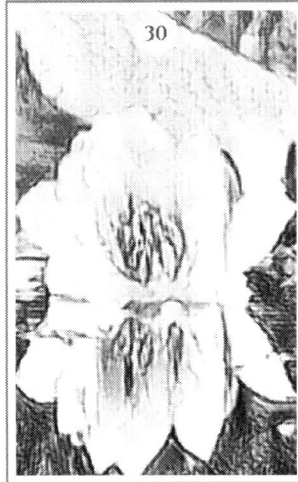

Playing Card	**King of Spades**
General (Noun)	Age, Maturity, Senior, Older Person, Older Man, Experience
General (adj)	Old, Mature, Ageing, Older, Wise, Experienced, Traditional
Love:	Mature Person, Older or Lifelong Love, Love Later in Life
Career:	Senior, Experienced Person, Retirement, Work With Elderly
People:	Mature, Experienced. Older & Wiser. Older relatives.
Timing	Thirty Days, Thirtieth of the Month. A Long Time. Winter.

Card's Message

Wisdom, maturity and experience are the key here. Take advice if you need it or trust your long experience. Be patient; think long-term.

Lily Card Combinations

LILY & RIDER: MATURITY; ONSET OF OLD AGE; ARRIVAL OF OLDER PERSON

LILY & CLOVER: LUCK COMES WITH WISDOM; LATER-LIFE GOOD FORTUNE;

LILY & SHIP: TRAVELLING OLDER PERSON; FOREIGN SENIOR CITIZEN

LILY & HOUSE: HEAD OF THE FAMILY; HOUSEBOUND OLDER PERSON

LILY & TREE: OLD AGE HEALTH ISSUES; HEALTHY OLD AGE; SPIRITUAL PEACE

LILY & CLOUDS   CONFUSED SENIOR; DEMENTIA

LILY & SNAKE: PROBLEMS OF OLD AGE; UNTRUSTWORTHY OLDER PERSON

LILY & COFFIN: END OF LIFE ISSUES; END OF WISDOM

LILY & BOUQUET: HAPPY OLD AGE; BLOOMING MATURITY; LATE BLOOMER

LILY & SCYTHE: SURGERY FOR OLDER PERSON; DECISIVE OLDER PERSON

LILY & WHIP: DIFFICULT SENIOR; TOUGH MENTOR; STRUGGLES OF OLD AGE

LILY & BIRDS: OLDER COUPLE; VERBAL ADVICE; TALKATIVE SENIOR

LILY & CHILD: YOUTHFUL OLDER PERSON; LATE STARTER; ELDEST CHILD

LILY & FOX: WORK SENIORITY; WORK EXPERIENCE; WILY OLD FOX

LILY & BEAR: POWERFUL ELDER; PROTECTIVE FATHER FIGURE

LILY & STARS: ESTABLISHED STAR; HIGH-FLYING SENIOR

LILY & STORKS: LATE STARTER; FRESH START FOR SENIOR

LILY & DOG: LIFELONG FRIEND; FRIENDLY OLDER PERSON

LILY & TOWER: ESTABLISHMENT; OLD ORDER; HIGH-RANKING OLDER PERSON

LILY & GARDEN: PUBLIC PARK; GROUP OF SENIORS

LILY & MOUNTAIN: ISOLATED OLDER PERSON; RIGID OLDER PERSON

LILY & CROSSROAD: CHOICES OF OLD AGE; MATURE OPTIONS

LILY & MICE: ANXIOUS SENIOR; STRESSFUL OLD AGE

LILY & HEART: LOVING OLDER PERSON; LIFE-LONG LOVE; LIFE'S PASSION

LILY & RING: LONG-TERM RELATIONSHIP; OLD BOND; MARRIED ELDER

LILY & BOOK: WISE ELDER; LIFE'S KNOWLEDGE; LONG-HELD SECRET

LILY & LETTER: NEWS OF AN OLDER PERSON

LILY & MAN: OLDER MAN; MALE MATURITY

LILY & WOMAN: OLDER WOMAN; FEMALE MATURITY

LILY & SUN: LATER IN LIFE SUCCESS; HAPPY OLD AGE

LILY & MOON: EMOTIONAL MATURITY; CREATIVE COMING-OF-AGE

LILY & KEY: IMPORTANT OLDER PERSON; SIGNIFICANT WISDOM

LILY & FISH: BUSINESS MATURITY; BUSINESS MENTOR

LILY & ANCHOR: LONG AND STABLE LIFE; SECURE OLD AGE

LILY & CROSS: TROUBLED OLD AGE; DIFFICULTY IN LATER YEARS

31. SUN

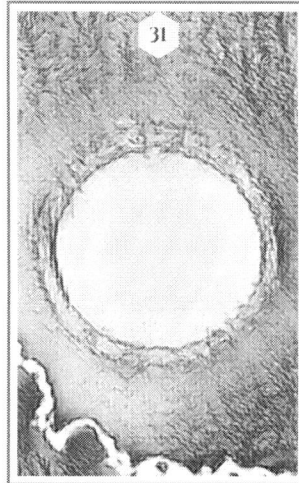

Playing Card	**Ace of Diamonds**
General (Noun)	Success, Happiness, Win, Victory, Light, Positivity
General (Adj)	Successful, Happy, Victorious, Winning, Joyful, Positive
Love	Happiness and joy. A successful relationship or partnership.
Career	Success and Achievement. Reputation. Endeavours Succeed
People	Positive, Successful People, Sunny Disposition, Confident
Timing:	Thirty-One days, A Month, 31st, Daytime. Dawn. Summer

Card's Message

Be positive; success and happiness is assured. Look for the good in everything; shine a light on truth. Confidence is all. Victory in your grasp.

Sun Card Combinations

SUN & RIDER: VICTORY; SUCCESS IS COMING

SUN & CLOVER: VERY SUCCESSFUL; GREAT OUTCOME; UNEXPECTED SUCCESS

SUN & SHIP: TRAVEL TO HOT COUNTRY; SUMMER HOLIDAY

SUN & HOUSE: DOMESTIC HAPPINESS; FAMILY SUCCESS

SUN & TREE: GOOD HEALTH; SPIRITUAL HAPPINESS

SUN & CLOUDS   MARRED SUCCESS; UNCERTAIN VICTORY

SUN & SNAKE: PROBLEMATIC SUCCESS; NOT AS GOOD AS IT LOOKED; ENVY

SUN & COFFIN: END OF A SUCCESSFUL PERIOD; POSITIVITY ENDS

SUN & BOUQUET: HAPPINESS AND JOY; CELEBRATION; AWARD

SUN & SCYTHE   SUDDEN SUCCESS; HAPPINESS IS SHORT-LIVED

SUN & WHIP: VICTORY; SUCCESS BRINGS STRAIN; CHALLENGING SUCCESS

SUN & BIRDS: POSITIVE TALK; MEETING SUCCESS; GOOD CONVERSATION

SUN & CHILD: CHILD'S HAPPINESS; CHILD'S ACHIEVEMENT; SMALL SUCCESS

SUN & FOX: SUCCESS AT WORK; WORK HAPPINESS; CLEVERNESS

SUN & BEAR: FINANCIAL SUCCESS; PROTECTIVE POSITIVITY

SUN & STARS: BIG ACHIEVEMENT; FAME; HOPES OF SUCCESS; SHINING STAR

SUN & STORKS   POSITIVE NEW START; GOOD PROGRESS

SUN & DOG: POSITIVE FRIENDSHIP; FRIEND'S HAPPINESS; FRIEND'S SUCCESS

SUN & TOWER	HIGH STATUS ACHIEVEMENT; ESTABLISHED SUCCESS
SUN & GARDEN:	GROUP ACHIEVEMENT; TEAM VICTORY; SOCIAL SUCCESS
SUN & MOUNTAIN:	OBSTACLES TO ACHIEVEMENT; BLOCKS TO HAPPINESS
SUN & CROSSROAD:	MULTIPLE ACHIEVEMENTS; POSITIVE CHOICE
SUN & MICE:	IMPOSTER SYNDROME; STRESSFUL ACHIEVEMENT
SUN & HEART:	LOVE AND HAPPINESS; ROMANTIC SUCCESS
SUN & RING:	HAPPY MARRIAGE; SUCCESSFUL PARTNERSHIP
SUN & BOOK:	SECRET JOY; UNKNOWN HAPPINESS; SUCCESSFUL EDUCATION
SUN & LETTER:	MESSAGE OF POSITIVITY; EMPOWERING MOTTO
SUN & MAN:	MAN'S ACHIEVEMENT; MAN'S SUCCESS; MAN'S HAPPINESS
SUN & WOMAN:	WOMAN'S ACHIEVEMENT; SUCCESS; WOMAN'S HAPPINESS
SUN & LILY:	LATE-IN-LIFE SUCCESS; HAPPINESS; HAPPY OLD AGE
SUN & MOON:	CREATIVE SUCCESS; EMOTIONAL POSITIVITY
SUN & KEY:	SIGNIFICANT ACHIEVEMENT; FATED SUCCESS
SUN & FISH:	BUSINESS SUCCESS; BUSINESS POSITIVITY
SUN & ANCHOR:	SETTLED AND HAPPY; LONG TERM SUCCESS
SUN & CROSS:	PRESSURED SUCCESS; WEIGHED DOWN BY ACHIEVEMENTS

32. MOON

Playing Card	**Eight of Hearts**
General (Noun)	Adulation ,Emotions, Intuition, Manifesting, Creativity, Mood,
General (Adj)	Creative, Emotional, Moody, Intuitive, Perceptive, Subjective
Love	Romantic Feelings, Adoration, Swept Up in Feelings, In Love
Career	Creative Jobs, The Arts, Holistic or Psychic, Intuitive Work
People	Creatives, Psychics, Empathetic, Moodiness, Sensitive
Timing	Lunar Cycle, Tidal, Evening, Night

Card's Message

Trust your intuition. Find time to create, purely for the joy of creating. What messages might your dreams be sending? Go with the flow, life's natural rhythms. Listen to your feelings.

Moon Card Combinations

Moon & Rider: PERIOD OF CREATIVITY; EMOTIONAL VISITOR; NEW ROMANCE

Moon & Clover: LUCKY INSTINCT; POSITIVE FEELINGS; ROMANTIC HAPPINESS

Moon & Ship   EMOTIONAL TRIP; UP-AND-DOWN FEELINGS; HONEYMOON

Moon & House: HOMESICKNESS; EMOTIONS CONNECTED WITH HOME

Moon & Tree   PSYCHIC; BUDDING CREATIVITY; EMOTIONAL HEALTH

Moon & Clouds: CONFUSED FEELINGS; MIXED EMOTIONS;

Moon & Snake: BETRAYED; UNPLEASANT FEELINGS; SENSE OF DANGER

Moon & Coffin: DEPRESSION; EMOTIONAL BLANKNESS; SHOCK

Moon & Bouquet: LOVELY FEELINGS; JOY; HAPPY EMOTIONS; VISUAL ART

Moon & Scythe: HURT FEELINGS; SUDDEN EMOTION; CUT OFF FEELINGS

Moon & Whip: DIFFICULT EMOTIONS; CHALLENGING FEELINGS

Moon & Birds: TALKING ABOUT FEELINGS; THERAPY; CREATIVE TALK

Moon & Child: CHILD'S EMOTIONS; KIDS' CREATIVITY; EARLY FEELINGS

Moon & Fox: FEELINGS OF DISTRUST; WORK-RELATED EMOTIONS

Moon & Bear   POWERFUL EMOTIONS; PROTECTIVE FEELING

Moon & Stars: DREAMS; DRAMA; FAMOUS CREATIVITY OR ARTISTRY

Moon & Storks: EMOTIONAL NEW START; NEW FEELINGS

Moon & Dog: FRIENDLY FEELINGS; PARTNER'S EMOTIONS; SOULMATE

MOON & TOWER:	TOP CREATIVITY; SNOBBY FEELINGS; EMOTIONAL ISOLATION
MOON & GARDEN:	GROUP EMOTIONS; PUBLIC DISPLAY OF EMOTION
MOON & MOUNTAIN:	BLOCKED FEELINGS; CREATIVE BLOCK
MOON & CROSSROAD:	CHOICE OF EMOTIONS; MANY DIFFERENT FEELINGS
MOON & MICE	ANXIOUS FEELINGS; HIGHLY-STRUNG; STRESS
MOON & HEART:	LOVING FEELINGS; PASSIONATE EMOTIONS
MOON & RING	CREATIVE CONTRACT; ART PAYMENT; LINKED EMOTIONS
MOON & BOOK:	SECRET FEELINGS; EMOTIONAL INTELLIGENCE; NOVEL
MOON & LETTER:	CREATIVE WRITING; POETRY; EMOTIONAL MESSAGE
MOON & MAN:	MALE EMOTIONS; MAN'S FEELINGS; MAN'S CREATIVITY
MOON & WOMAN:	FEMALE EMOTIONS; FEELINGS; WOMAN'S CREATIVITY
MOON & LILY:	MATURE EMOTIONS; FULLY-DEVELOPED CREATIVITY
MOON & SUN:	POSITIVE EMOTIONS; HAPPY ROMANCE; CREATIVE SUCCESS
MOON & KEY:	SIGNIFICANT FEELINGS; IMPORTANT SIGN; GUT FEELING
MOON & FISH:	BUSINESS SENSE; CREATIVE BUSINESS; FEELINGS OF FREEDOM
MOON & ANCHOR:	STABLE EMOTIONS; LONG TERM FEELINGS
MOON & CROSS:	DEPRESSION; HEAVY FEELINGS; EMOTIONAL BURDENS

33. KEY

Playing Card	**Eight of Diamonds**
General (Noun)	Key, Answer, Fate, Significance, Importance, Destiny, Solution
General (Adj):	Significant, Fated, Important, Major, Destined, Key, Crucial
Love:	The One, Soulmate, Meant To Be, Love Of Your Life
Career	Importance, Solution, Crucial points, Significant Individual
People:	Important, Destined People, Movers & Shakers, Influencers
Timing:	Now. Eternal. All Time.

Card's Message

The answer, the solution arrives. Yes! What will be will be; fate and destiny calls.

KEY CARD COMBINATIONS

KEY & RIDER: KEY EVENT; IMPORTANT VISITOR; SOMETHING BIG COMING

KEY & CLOVER: FATED LUCK; LUCKY KARMA; SIGNIFICANT GOOD FORTUNE

KEY & SHIP: IMPORTANT JOURNEY; TRIP OF A LIFETIME; DESTINY

KEY & HOUSE: HOUSE KEY; TRUE NORTH; IMPORTANT HOUSE

KEY & TREE: SPIRITUAL SIGNIFICANCE; KARMIC FORCES; HEALTH ANSWER

KEY & CLOUDS: UNCERTAIN FATE; ANSWER UNCLEAR; HIDDEN SIGNIFICANCE

KEY & SNAKE: ILL-FATED; NEGATIVE ANSWER; LIES; BAD KARMA; DANGER

KEY & COFFIN: IMPORTANT ENDING; FINAL ANSWER; BIG LIFE CHANGE

KEY & BOUQUET: SIGNIFICANT GIFT; POSITIVE DESTINY; BLESSED

KEY & SCYTHE   IMPORTANT DECISION; TURNING POINT; FATED DECISION

KEY & WHIP: BIG ARGUMENT; KEY CONFLICT; FATED CHALLENGE

KEY & BIRDS: IMPORTANT CONVERSATION; NECESSARY COMMUNICATION

KEY & CHILD: SIGNIFICANT CHILD; IMPORTANT BEGINNINGS

KEY & FOX: JOB IMPORTANCE; DEEPLY UNTRUSTWORTHY

KEY & BEAR: FINANCIAL KEY; PROTECTIVE KARMA; POWERFUL DESTINY

KEY & STARS: DESTINED TO BE KNOWN; GOALS WILL BE ACHIEVED

KEY & STORKS: FRESH START NEEDED; FATED NEW BEGINNING

KEY & DOG: SIGNIFICANT FRIEND; SOULMATE; FATED COMPANION

KEY & TOWER: OFFICIAL IMPORTANCE; AT THE HIGHEST LEVEL

KEY & GARDEN: PUBLIC SIGNIFICANCE; SHARED ANSWER; IMPORTANT EVENT

KEY & MOUNTAIN: SIGNIFICANT OBSTACLE; FATED DELAY

KEY & CROSSROAD: SIGNIFICANT LIFE CHOICES; CHOOSE WELL

KEY & MICE: SIGNIFICANT CONCERNS; IMPORTANT WORRIES

KEY & HEART: ROMANTIC FATE; LOVE DESTINY; SIGNIFICANT ROMANCE

KEY & RING: IMPORTANT CONTRACT; FATED LINK; KEY RELATIONSHIP

KEY & BOOK: THE ANSWER; FORTUNE TELLING; SIGNIFICANT KNOWLEDGE

KEY & LETTER: WRITTEN ANSWER; IMPORTANT MESSAGE

KEY & MAN: SIGNIFICANT MAN; SOULMATE; MAN'S DESTINY

KEY & WOMAN: SIGNIFICANT WOMAN; SOULMATE; WOMAN'S DESTINY

KEY & LILY: EXPERIENCE KEY; IMPORTANT OLDER PERSON; MENTOR

KEY & SUN: BIG SUCCESS; HUGE ACHIEVEMENT; SUCCESS IS ASSURED

KEY & MOON: CORE FEELINGS; SENSE OF SIGNIFICANCE; PSYCHIC FEELINGS

KEY & FISH: BUSINESS FATE; KEY TO THE BUSINESS

KEY & ANCHOR: LONG-TERM FATE; DESTINY; THE ONLY ANSWER

KEY & CROSS: RELIGIOUS CONVERSION; TROUBLED FATE; GUILT

34. FISH

Playing Card	**King of Diamonds**
General (Noun)	Business, Independence, Freedom, Adaptability, Cashflow
General (Adj)	Business-Related, Independent, Freedom-Loving, Adaptable
Love	Free Agent, Independent, Happily Single, No-Strings
Career:	Business, Freelancing, Entrepreneurs, Small Business, Sales
People:	Independent, Go With The Flow, Freedom-Loving, Solo
Timing:	n/a

Card's Message

Go with the flow; maintain your independence and freedom. Be enterprising. Abundance in all that you do.

Fish Card Combinations

Fish & Rider:	BUSINESS ARRIVAL ON THE SCENE; BUSINESS NEWS
Fish & Clover:	LUCKY BUSINESS; BUSINESS OPPORTUNITY; GOOD FORTUNE
Fish & Ship:	OVERSEAS BUSINESS; TRAVEL BUSINESS; TRADE
Fish & House:	WORKING FROM HOME; DOMESTIC BUSINESS; FAMILY WORK
Fish & Tree:	HEALTH SERVICES; SPIRITUAL BUSINESS; GROWING BUSINESS
Fish & Clouds:	UNCLEAR BUSINESS; UNCERTAIN WORK
Fish & Snake	DODGY BUSINESS; UNTRUSTWORTHY, SLIPPERY.
Fish & Coffin:	UNDERTAKERS; FUNERAL BUSINESS; BUSINESS ENDING
Fish & Bouquet:	BEAUTY BUSINESS; FLORIST; PLEASANT BUSINESS
Fish & Scythe:	BUSINESS CUTS; DENTIST; BUSINESS DECISIONS
Fish & Whip:	COACHING, TRAINING WORK; SPORTS BUSINESS
Fish & Birds:	PRESS OFFICE; COMMS BUSINESS; VOICEOVER WORK
Fish & Child:	WORKING WITH CHILDREN; NANNY
Fish & Fox:	CORPORATE WORK; EMPLOYED; UNDERHAND BUSINESS
Fish & Bear:	FINANCIAL BUSINESS; BODYBUILDING; FOOD INDUSTRY
Fish & Stars:	AGENT; CELEBRITY WORK; AMBITIOUS BUSINESS
Fish & Storks:	NEW BUSINESS; BUSINESS CHANGES; STARTUP
Fish & Dog:	BUSINESS PARTNERSHIP; WORKING WITH SOMEONE YOU KNOW

FISH & TOWER: OFFICIAL BUSINESS; CORPORATE CONTRACTOR; LEGAL WORK

FISH & GARDEN: PUBLIC WORK; PUBLIC RELATIONS; PARTY PLANNER

FISH & MOUNTAIN: BLOCKED BUSINESS; FREEDOM CURTAILED

FISH & CROSSROAD: MULTIPLE BUSINESSES; CHOICE OF WORK; CHOICE OF BUSINESS

FISH & MICE: STRESSFUL WORK; BUSINESS WORRIES

FISH & HEART: PASSIONATE JOB; DATING AGENCY

FISH & RING: WORKING ON CONTRACTS; BUSINESS PARTNERSHIP; MERGER

FISH & BOOK: PUBLISHING; ACADEMIC WORK

FISH & LETTER   FREELANCE WRITING; JOURNALISM

FISH & MAN: BUSINESSMAN; MAN'S BUSINESS; BUSINESS FOR MALES

FISH & WOMAN: BUSINESSWOMAN; WOMAN'S BUSINESS; BUSINESS FOR WOMEN

FISH & LILY: MATURE BUSINESS; WORK WITH OLDER PEOPLE; CONSULTANT

FISH & SUN: SUCCESSFUL BUSINESS; ESCAPE

FISH & MOON: CREATIVE WORK; EMOTION-RELATED BUSINESS

FISH & KEY: SIGNIFICANT BUSINESS; IMPORTANT CAREER

FISH & ANCHOR: LONG-TERM BUSINESS; STABLE BUSINESS; LONG-TERM FREEDOM

FISH & CROSS: COUNSELLING WORK; SPIRITUAL WORKER; THERAPIST

35. ANCHOR

Playing Card	**Nine of Spades**
General (Noun)	Stability, Permanence, Security, Safety, Solidity, Reliability
General (Adj)	Stable, Reliable, Long-Term, Secure, Safe, Permanent, Grounded
Love:	Secure, Committed Relationship, Safe, Long-Term, Lasting.
Career	Stable Career, Solid Prospects, Job security. Naval.
People:	Reliable, Secure, Solid, Emotionally Stable, Sensible. Reassuring.
Timing:	Lifelong, a Lifetime. Forever.

Card's Message

Security and permanence is key. Stick to your guns, persevere. Keep things stable and go for the long-term options. In it for the long haul.

ANCHOR CARD COMBINATIONS

ANCHOR & RIDER: STABILITY ARRIVES; A SENSE OF PERMANENCE

ANCHOR & CLOVER: CERTAIN GOOD FORTUNE; LASTING LUCK

ANCHOR & SHIP: LONG JOURNEY; HARBOUR; MOORED

ANCHOR & HOUSE: DOMESTIC STABILITY; PERMANENT HOME; STABLE FAMILY

ANCHOR & TREE: LONG-TERM HEALTH; LONGEVITY; SPIRITUAL CORE

ANCHOR & CLOUDS: UNSETTLED; UNCLEAR WHAT IS NEEDED; UPROOTED

ANCHOR & SNAKE: LONG-TERM PROBLEMS; DANGER

ANCHOR & COFFIN: STABILITY ENDS; FINALITY

ANCHOR & BOUQUET: CONTENTMENT; HAPPILY SETTLED; COMFORTABLE

ANCHOR & SCYTHE: SUDDEN CHANGES; RUG PULLED FROM UNDER YOUR FEET

ANCHOR & WHIP: LONG-TERM HARDSHIP; ADDICTION; CONSTANT STRUGGLE

ANCHOR & BIRDS: LONG CONVERSATION; LIFELONG COMPANION

ANCHOR & CHILD: FOREVER CHILDLIKE; STUBBORNNESS

ANCHOR & FOX: WORK STABILITY; PERMANENT JOB

ANCHOR & BEAR: FINANCIAL STABILITY; PROTECTION AND SAFETY

ANCHOR & STARS: LONG-TERM AMBITIONS; ACHIEVING GOALS

ANCHOR & STORKS: STABLE NEW START; PERMANENT CHANGE

ANCHOR & DOG: LOYALTY; STEADFASTNESS; LONG-TERM FRIENDSHIP

ANCHOR & TOWER: RIGIDITY; IMPERIOUSNESS; PRISON

ANCHOR & GARDEN: GROUP STABILITY; LONG-TERM NETWORK

ANCHOR & MOUNTAIN   STAGNATION; STUCK OR BLOCKED FROM MOVING ON

ANCHOR & CROSSROAD: UNCOMMITTED; KEEPING OPTIONS OPEN

ANCHOR & MICE: CLINGINESS; DEPENDENCE; ANXIOUS ATTACHMENT

ANCHOR & HEART: STABLE ROMANCE; LONG-TERM LOVE

ANCHOR & RING: COMMITMENT; STABLE MARRIAGE; LONG-TERM PARTNERSHIP

ANCHOR & BOOK: STALLED LEARNING; STUCK IN THEIR WAYS

ANCHOR & LETTER: WRITTEN COMMITMENT; SIGNATURE

ANCHOR & MAN: RELIABLE MAN; STUBBORN MAN

ANCHOR & WOMAN: RELIABLE WOMAN; STUBBORN WOMAN

ANCHOR & LILY: VINTAGE; ROOTS; LIFELONG STABILITY

ANCHOR & SUN: LONG-TERM HAPPINESS; STABLE SUCCESS

ANCHOR & MOON: EMOTIONAL STABILITY; CREATIVE HUB

ANCHOR & KEY: LONG-TERM SUCCESS; IMPORTANT STABILITY

ANCHOR & FISH: BUSINESS STABILITY; LONGSTANDING BUSINESS

ANCHOR & CROSS: LONG-TERM TROUBLES; WEIGHTY ISSUES

36. CROSS

Playing Card	**Six of Clubs**
General (Noun)	Burdens, Troubles, Weighty Issues, Depression, Religion, Ordeal
General (Adj)	Burdened, Troubled, Weighed-Down, Dogmatic
Love	Self-Sacrifice, Codependence, Pressurised, Obligations, Duty
Career:	High-pressure, Responsibilities, Burdens. Therapy, Priesthood
People:	Religious, Martyrs, Troubled, Depressed Guilt-Ridden, Weary
Timing:	Long-Lasting

Card's Message

What is troubling or weighing you down right now? Can you talk to others to ease the burden? Are you taking care of you? Remember that you can't take care of others if you aren't looking after yourself. Get the help and support you need.

CROSS CARD COMBINATIONS

CROSS & RIDER: HARD TIME AHEAD; RELIGIOUS REVIVAL; PRESSURE COMING

CROSS & CLOVER: PROBLEMS RESOLVE; TROUBLES BRING LUCK

CROSS & SHIP: PROBLEMS ON A JOURNEY; TROUBLED TRIP; OVERSEAS ISSUES

CROSS & HOUSE: FAMILY TROUBLES; DOMESTIC ISSUES; HOUSE PROBLEMS

CROSS & TREE   HEALTH PROBLEMS; SPIRITUAL CRISIS

CROSS & CLOUDS: MENTAL HEALTH ISSUES; DEMENTIA; SERIOUS CONFUSION

CROSS & SNAKE: SERIOUS DIFFICULTIES; UPSET OVER BETRAYAL; CRISIS

CROSS & COFFIN: FUNERAL; THE END OF TROUBLES

CROSS & BOUQUET: BEAUTY ISSUES; TROUBLED APPEARANCE; LIGHT BURDENS

CROSS & SCYTHE: ACCIDENT; HARD DECISION; PROBLEMS SWIFTLY RESOLVE

CROSS & WHIP: ABUSE; VIOLENCE; OVER- PRESSURED; SEXUAL DIFFICULTIES

CROSS & BIRDS: DIFFICULT COMMUNICATION; HEAVY TALK; VERBAL PRESSURE

CROSS & CHILD: HEAVILY PREGNANT; KID PROBLEMS; TROUBLED YOUNGSTER

CROSS & FOX: SEVERE PRESSURE AT WORK; UNDERHANDED PROBLEM

CROSS & BEAR   FINANCIAL DIFFICULTIES; HEAVY RESPONSIBILITY

CROSS & STARS: THE PROBLEMS OF FAME; ACHIEVEMENT BRINGS DIFFICULTIES

CROSS & STORKS: DIFFICULT NEW START; FRESH BEGINNINGS AFTER HARDSHIP

CROSS & DOG: COUNSELLING, MORAL SUPPORT; HELPING OUT

CROSS & TOWER: PROBLEMS WITH OFFICIALS; RELIGIOUS BURDENS; GUILT

CROSS & GARDEN: PUBLIC PRESSURE; SHARED TROUBLES; SUPPORT GROUP

CROSS & MOUNTAIN: PROBLEMS PREVENTED; DEPRESSION & ISOLATION; DELAYS

CROSS & CROSSROAD: MULTIPLE BURDENS; NO EASY CHOICES

CROSS & MICE   SERIOUS STRESS, DEPRESSION, ANXIETY; UNDER PRESSURE

CROSS & HEART: ROMANTIC TROUBLES; DIFFICULT LOVE LIFE

CROSS & RING   RESTRICTIVE RELATIONSHIP; BURDENSOME PARTNERSHIP;

CROSS & BOOK: LEARNING DIFFICULTIES; SECRET TROUBLES; BIBLE

CROSS & LETTER: UPSETTING NEWS; RELIGIOUS WRITINGS

CROSS & MAN: MAN'S TROUBLES; STRESSED MAN; MARTYR

CROSS & WOMAN: WOMAN'S TROUBLES; STRESSED WOMAN; MARTYR

CROSS & LILY: THE PROBLEMS OF OLD AGE; WEIGHED DOWN BY EXPERIENCE

CROSS & SUN: SUCCESS AFTER A TROUBLED TIME; EVENTUAL HAPPINESS

CROSS & MOON: EMOTIONALLY TROUBLED; CREATIVE DIFFICULTIES

CROSS & KEY: SPIRITUAL CRISIS; FUTURE TROUBLES

CROSS & FISH   BUSINESS TROUBLES; CASHFLOW ISSUES

CROSS & ANCHOR: LONG TERM DIFFICULTIES; DEPRESSION; HEAVY BURDEN

II

LENORMAND CARD LAYOUTS

Card Layouts – Basics

Just as in the Tarot system, there are a number of commonly-used layouts in Lenormand. But how do you know which layout or spread is going to be best to use in your particular situation?

In answering that, you need to first think about these questions:

❖ What kind of information are you looking to get from the reading?
♣ Is your reading general or specific?
❖ How much detail would you like from the reading?
♣ What's the timeframe you want to look at?

OVERVIEW OF CARD LAYOUTS & THEIR USES

The following are some of the main layouts readers use in the Lenormand system.

SINGLE CARD

It's not really a layout, but people often do use single cards, particularly in daily practice, in personal Lenormand journals and so on. Personally, I get more out of Lenormand from using the cards in combination. but have on occasion used them singly.

Use for:

❖ Daily readings - Card for the Day, or Coming Up Today
❖ The overall theme or vibe of a situation

✤ Musing on a card's meaning, message and particular relevance in your life. This is particularly useful when you are first learning the Lenormand Card Meanings.

3-CARD SPREAD

This is the simplest layout you can do and particularly useful for practice if you are new to Lenormand Card Combinations.

Use for:

✤ Brief overviews of a situation with the centre card as a keycard.
✤ Simple Past-Present-Future readings
✤ Daily personal readings and Lenormand journaling.

NB Take the meanings down a notch if you're using in daily readings. Used on a daily basis, they are usually fairly gentle and undramatic.

5-CARD SPREAD (LINE OF 5)

My personal favourite in my regular practice, because it is both simple AND gives a fair amount of detail. You can use either with a key card at the centre to focus the reading on a pre-ordained topic, or without a key card for what is often a more accurate general reading or answer to a question. It requires the use of card combinations. I use this layout every week in my own personal Weekly Readings.

Use for:

✤ A good, quick, overview of a situation with all the most important details included
✤ Focused readings with a key card
✤ General readings without a key card
✤ Weekly readings

9-CARD SPREAD (3x3)

I also use this fairly regularly, but where my 5-Card Spread would be my main overview, this one is my focus reading. I rarely use it without a key card at the centre and I use it mainly to go more in depth and get more detail about a situation or person. This often happens when something - or someone - comes up in a 5-card reading that I have more questions about. This reading requires using card combinations and is less about timing than it is about focus.

Use for:

✤ Focus, with a key card, on a situation, specific life area, or person.
✤ Exploratory or investigative readings, to get more detail and information
✤ Unearthing hidden or important factors in a situation or about someone
✤ Readings where getting as much information as possible is important.
✤ Situations where you also want an idea of how the past will feed into the future.
✤ People readings and biographical and personal detail
✤ A section of a Grand Tableau reading (see below)

THE GRAND TABLEAU

This is the big one, and is a highly complex, integrated reading using all 36 cards. It is also never quick to do, so it isn't one to do often.

It should never cover a period of less than a month, and personally I find even that too short, but is great for big long-term timeframes such as annual readings. It's extremely detailed, holds an enormous amount of information, and will give you details of every single aspect of a person's life and situation.

You can make it as complex as you want, reading every single card in detail, looking at the main trends, or just focus on particular life areas using the 9-card technique within the spread. You can also utilise more advanced techniques in the Grand Tableau, such as mirroring, reflection and knighting.

Use for:

- ✤ General personal readings, then honing in on specific life areas within the spread.
- ✤ Long-term timeframes of a month or more
- ✤ Annual readings
- ✤ In-depth detail and exploration; every aspect of a person's life
- ✤ A high level of detail about past and future influences

A NOTE ABOUT USING TAROT SPREADS WITH LENORMAND

What about mixing Lenormand with Tarot spreads, like the Celtic Cross?

You can if you like, and I used to read Tarot cards all the time, but I'm not personally a fan of mixing the two systems in terms of spreads because the spreads are designed to work best with that system.

Tarot and Lenormand are like apples and oranges; both are good, but taste different. I have seen people combine the cards successfully but only in very specific situations where they want both of the aspects that the two different card-reading systems offer.

Remember, Lenormand is the universal day-to-day life stuff and is very grounded, earth-bound and direct. It's like a wise older relative shaking their finger at you and telling you what's what. Tarot is much more esoteric, new age and spiritual in nature and is more suitable for those who want to incorporate its truths as part of a long-term inner spiritual journey.

Which Lenormand Card Layout Should I Use?

LAYOUT	TIME FRAME	USE FOR
1-CARD	**Daily**	• Card of the Day • Overall Theme • Quick Answer • Learning Card Meanings
3-CARD	**Daily**	• Daily Journal • Simple Overview • Quick Past, Present, Future • Beginning Learning Card Combinations
5-CARD	**Weekly**	• Overview with Main Details • With or Without Keycard • Multi-Purpose • Learning Card Combinations
9-CARD	**Weekly +**	• Focus With Keycard • Explore Key Issues • Reveal Detail & Hidden Info • Past, Present, Future • People Info/Bio
GRAND TABLEAU	**Monthly +**	• All 36 Cards • In-Depth • Big Picture & Detail • Long-Term Readings • Explore All Life Areas • Reveal Hidden Info & Influences

3-CARD SPREAD

This is one of the simplest Lenormand readings you can do. It's suitable in particular for daily journal readings, or for when you need a very quick overview of a situation. You can also use it for basic Past, Present, Future readings.

I'll give you two different methods here for using a 3-card spread. Be sure to decide before you ask your question of the cards which of these two ways you're going to use them.

PAST—PRESENT—FUTURE

In this reading, you'll look at each card on its own and not use card combinations.

Step 1

Think of the situation you want to know more about and shuffle the cards. While you're shuffling, ask for the Past, Present and Future of that situation.

Step 2

When the cards feel right to you, pull out three cards.

Different readers have different methods for pulling cards: please use the method you normally use and that feels right to you. I tend to shuffle until I "know" it's time to stop, and then I pull out one card and those either side of it. Others may shuffle and pull three cards randomly; still others may cut the cards as you would for Tarot and take the top three. Whatever works for you.

Lay out the cards from left to right, as below:

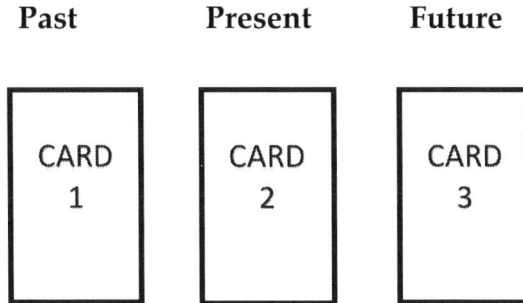

Past   **Present**   **Future**

CARD 1	CARD 2	CARD 3

Step 3

Read Card 1 as the past of the situation, Card 2 as the present, Card 3 as the future. In this version of the reading, you don't combine the cards.

EXAMPLE

Q: What Is The Past, Present & Future of This Love Relationship?

I pull the following three cards in relation to this question.

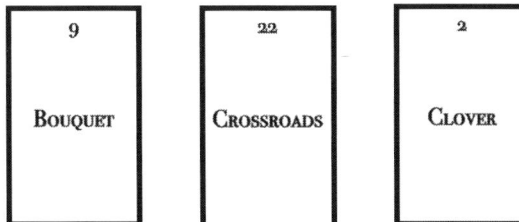

9	22	2
BOUQUET	CROSSROADS	CLOVER

I then read the cards as follows:

The past of this situation: There's been something lovely and pleasant, maybe even a wedding.

The situation now: Now there are options. The relationship is at a turning point.

The situation in the future: The future of this situation looks lucky and positive.

As you see, it's a very simple way to read the cards. It doesn't give a huge amount of information or depth, but is clear and direct.

3-CARD SPREAD: LINKED READING

This is how I would normally read the cards, and is more like other Lenormand readings in that it looks at the cards using combinations.

Again, be sure to decide in your head before you ask your question of the cards that this is the way you're going to read them.

Step 1

Think of the question you want to ask and shuffle the cards. You don't need to choose a themed keycard for the spread (like the Heart for love, for instance) although you can choose one if you wish. If you do, it will be the centre card.

Step 2

When the cards feel right to you, pull out your three cards and lay them out from left to right, as below.

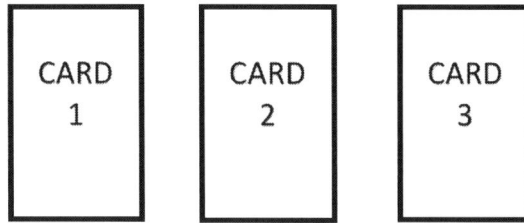

Step 3

First look at the cards individually.

Then read the centre card as the core of the situation you've asked about, followed by Cards 1+3 together in combination. This gives you the heart of the issue and what surrounds it.

Step 4

Then read the other pairs of cards in combinations as follows:

Cards 1+2, Cards 2+3. This tells the "story" of the reading, moving broadly from the past into the future.

EXAMPLE

Q: What Are The Prospects For This Romance?

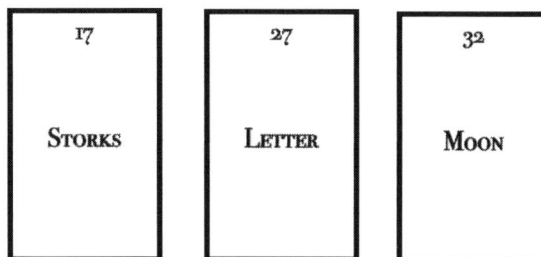

I look at the cards individually first. The cards show a new beginning (Storks), news, a letter or a message (Letter) and emotions or feelings (Moon).

The centre card of the reading is the **Letter**, so at the heart of the answer is that there's news or a message coming. The news is surrounded by **Storks + Moon**: an emotional or romantic new beginning. In other words: news of an emotional fresh start.

Then I read **Cards 1+2,** and then **2+ 3** together. This gives me:
A messaged or written   new start (**Storks + Letter**) and an emotional or romantic message (**Letter + Moon**)

Q: What Are The Prospects For This Romance?
A: It sounds as if it is early days, and perhaps the querent and their prospective love have been messaging one another. The querent should soon be receiving a romantic or emotional message.

5-CARD SPREAD (LINE OF 5)

This has become my go-to layout, as it gives me a quick and clear insight into pretty much anything I want to ask.

Essentially, you pick five cards, and lay them out in a row, the middle card usually being the focus of the reading. The only exception to this is if the Querent card appears elsewhere along the row. If this is the case, then you'll get clearer information if you use the Querent as the key card, regardless of position.

How to Pick Your Five Cards
I have two ways of picking them. In both cases, I shuffle the deck while holding the question I want answered in my mind. Generally, it is best to avoid 'yes' or 'no' type

questions; this is about details. Lenormand responds best to clear questions, as the answers can be very literal!

Either I pull the five cards out at random when shuffling while concentrating on the question I want to ask. This is known as "reading blind."

OR

If I already have a clear card 'focus' (money, job, opportunities, for example, or if I'm asking about a particular person) then after I've shuffled the cards and feel that the answer is 'ready', I find that representative card in the deck—again, this is known as using a **Keycard**—and along with it, pull out the cards that were either side of it in the pack to make my five.

I've had good results with both methods. Other readers will shuffle and cut the cards the way they might with Tarot. It really is up to you to do it the way that feels right to you. Either way, you should have a row of five cards laid out in front of you, as below.

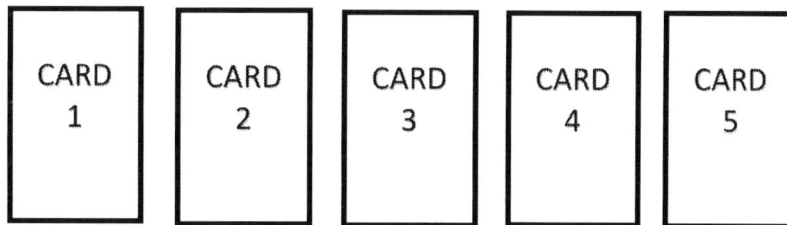

CARD 1	CARD 2	CARD 3	CARD 4	CARD 5

How To Read The Cards

First, read the cards **individually**, from left to right.

The **centre card** will give you the key issue in the reading (of course, if you've already chosen it as a focus card, then you'll already know what that is). NB see my exception above - if the Querent card appears in the line of five, you can use that as the starting point.

Then, for a good overview of the whole reading, read the following:

Cards 2+3, then **Cards 3+4** = The core of the reading
Cards 1+5, then **Cards 2+4** = The details surrounding it

Next, read the **cards in pairs**, going along the row from left to right, like a story:

Card 1 + Card 2
Card 2 + Card 3
Card 3 + Card 4
Card 4 + Card 5

In addition, I have found it can be helpful to add further to the detail by reading **all** the cards in pairs, so:

Cards 1 +2, 1 +3, 1+ 4, 1+5, for example. Then **2+3, 2+4, 2+5** etc.

You may get a few repetitions, but it stops you from missing out vital bits of information.

EXAMPLE

Question: What opportunities will be coming up for me this week?

I shuffle the deck thinking about this question and use the **Clover** card—representing luck, chance, opportunity —as the focus.

Cards 1-5 come out as follows:

12	17	2	34	33
BIRDS	STORKS	CLOVER	FISH	KEY

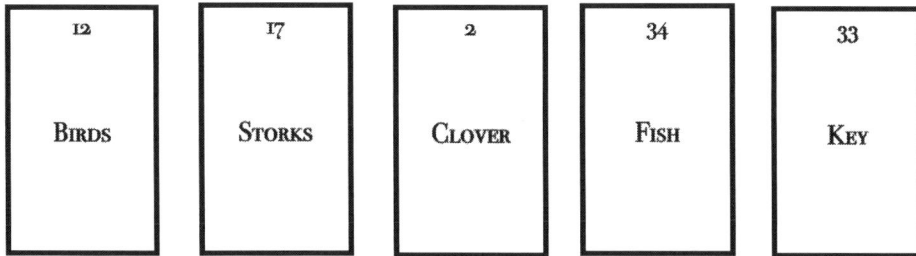

I already know that the Centre Card, Clover, represents **Opportunities**

Cards read individually:

Communication/Conversation; Fresh Start; Opportunity, Luck; Business; Importance

Overview of the whole reading:

Cards 2+3, then Cards 3+4 = Core of the reading
Storks-Clover, Clover-Fish = Lucky new start; business opportunity

Cards 1+5, then Cards 2+4 = Issues surrounding that
Birds-Key, Storks-Fish = Important conversation; A new beginning in business

Cards read in pairs, from left to right:

Card 1 + Card 2 = Birds + Storks = Change-making conversations or communication
Card 2 + Card 3 = Storks + Clover = Opportunity for a fresh start
Card 3 + Card 4 = Clover + Fish = Freelance business opportunity
Card 4 + Card 5 = Fish + Key = Important freelance business, vocation

So this indicates that my opportunities this week involve some kind of conversation or communication about a fresh start, perhaps the chance for a new business for myself that would be key and based around a vocation.

And for further detail about all the main elements:

Cards 1 + 2 = Birds + Storks = change-making conversations or communication
Card 1 + 3 = Birds + Clover = chance conversation or communication
Cards 1 + 4 = Birds + Fish = business conversation or communication
Cards 1 + 5 = Birds + Key = important conversation or communication

This is also telling me the communication itself is probably a 'chance' thing about business that will turn out to be key.

Card 2 + Card 3 = Storks + Clover = opportunity for a fresh start
Cards 2 + 4 = Storks + Fish = a new beginning in business
Cards 2 + 5 = Storks + Key = an important new beginning

The opportunity involved is not just any old new start, it could be the start of something major for me..

Card 3 + Card 4 = Clover + Fish = freelance business opportunity
Card 3 + Card 5 = Clover + Key = major opportunity, life-changing opportunity, lucky twist of fate

In other words, a business opportunity that should not be missed as it's a big deal

Card 4 + Card 5 = Fish + Key = important freelance business, vocation

The chance perhaps to make a business out of my vocation

So, in summary:
What opportunities will be coming up for me this week?

Answer:
My opportunities this week involve picking up on some kind of passing conversation or communication that could translate to a huge and potentially life-changing fresh start, most likely the creation of a new freelance business based around a vocation. It's a chance that I really shouldn't miss.

9-CARD (3x3) SPREAD

While I use the 5-card for most day-to-day readings, I tend to find the 9-card useful when I want more detail around a given situation, and have a little more time to go into it in depth.

How To Pick Your 9 Cards

Pretty much as per the 5-card spread. Again, I shuffle the cards holding the question I want answered in my mind, and pick the cards that feel right.

Because I generally tend to use this one to discover more about a given situation, I've usually chosen my key card beforehand. Once I've shuffled and get "the feeling" that I'm done, I stop and look for the keycard in the pack. Then I make it the centre of my reading (**Card 5** in the layout below) and take the cards that fall before and after it to form the rest.

However, I know not all readers do it this way. Some readers pick and lay the cards in order from 1-9 after shuffling and cutting the pack (or asking their client to do so).

It's also worth pointing out that even if you do know what you are focusing on, *not* having the keycard and doing a "blind" reading with whatever comes up can sometimes give you even better, sometimes unexpected, information.

However you prefer to do it, you want to end up with the cards laid out as follows:

CARD 1	CARD 2	CARD 3
CARD 4	CARD 5	CARD 6
CARD 7	CARD 8	CARD 9

How To Read The Cards

First, I take a general overview of the whole reading by reading the diamond around the centre card 5:

Card 2 +Card 4 + Card 8 + Card 6 = overview of this issue

Next for the reading proper.

You read the cards first as **horizontals:**

Card 1 + Card 2 + Card 3 = About this issue

Card 4 + Card 5 + Card 6 = The answer to the question asked

Card 7 + Card 8 + Card 9 = Additional or hidden information

And then the **vertical columns** from left to right, which represent the Past, the Present, and the Future:

Card 1 + Card 4 + Card 7= Recent past situation in relation to this issue

Card 2 + Card 5 + Card 8= Present situation in relation to this issue

Card 3 + Card 6 + Card 9= Near future situation in relation to this issue

Finally, I read the **diagonals** to get a sense of the development of this issue from the past into the future:

Card 1 + Card 5 + Card 9 then **Card 7 + Card 5 + Card 3**

EXAMPLE

Question: Helen is worried about money at the moment. What does she need to know about her current situation?

The cards fall as follows (see over):

1	28	34
RIDER	MAN	FISH

14	15	13
FOX	BEAR	CHILD

27	19	25
LETTER	TOWER	RING

General overview of the whole reading:

Card 2 +Card 4 + Card 8 + Card 6= Man + Fox + Tower + Child

Corporate male / deceitful male; "official" employee or deceiver; young organization

This has something to do with a male and with officialdom, perhaps a bank, and may involve deception.

Now the reading proper:

First, I read the horizontals:

About this issue

Card 1 + Card 2 + Card 3 = Rider + Man + Fish = Male visitor; business man; a business comes into play

The business interests of a male come into play

The answer to the question

Card 4 + Card 5 + Card 6 = Â Fox + bear + child = Financial deceit, finance worker; child's finances, child deceit or work

The Child possibly represents a customer here, although it could just be a young employee

A child's (customer's?) finances, work situation and salary, are possibly under suspicion

Additional information

Card 7 + Card 8 + Card 9 = Â Letter + Tower + Ring = Official letter; payment officialdom; payment letter/statement

A letter or document from an organisation about an agreement or payment

Next, we look at the vertical columns from left to right:

Recent past

Card 1 + Card 4 + Card 7 = Rider + Fox + Letter = work or deception news; offer of work or work documentation (or a fraud notification); a document arrives

A document or news arrives around work or deception

Present situation in relation to this issue

Card 2 + Card 5 + Card 8 = Man + Bear + Tower = financial male; bank; bank official

A male bank official and financial officialdom is very much in the picture

Near future situation in relation to this issue

Card 3 + Card 6 + Card 9 = Fish + Child + Ring = young, customer's business; deal, agreement; contracted customer

An agreement of some kind with the customer - perhaps a customer service agreement, or a payment.

Finally, let's take a look at the diagonals to get a sense of the development of this issue:

The development of this issue from past to future

Card 1 + Card 5 + Card 9 = Rider + Bear + Ring= the arrival of a payment

Card 7 + Card 5 + Card 3 = Letter + Bear + Fish = a business letter about finances

Money will arrive, as will a business letter about income sources.

So, in summary:

Q: Helen is worried about money at the moment. What does she need to know about her current situation?

A: Overall, the reading indicates there's something to do with a male official, perhaps the bank, and may involve deception. The business interests of this male are a factor. I think Helen is a customer of this institution and her finances, work situation and salary are possibly under suspicion. There are indications that there'll be a letter or statement from this institution about an agreement or payment.

It looks as though there has already been some kind of letter or notification of some kind about Helen's finances; perhaps a statement, a bank letter or a fraud notification, and now a male bank official is involved. It seems that in the future a payment is coming, to do with the customer's business, although it may be some kind of financial agreement. The reading indicates that some sort of written agreement or payment will arrive and a letter about finances

THE GRAND TABLEAU

The Grand Tableau is the daddy of Lenormand Readings and involves all 36 cards. It's a big and involved reading, very complex to do and can give you a huge amount of information about ANY aspect of the querent's life you want to explore.In terms of timeframe, we are looking pretty big-picture. It's a "What Will the Next Year Bring?" kind of reading.
You will find out exactly why this is when we go into the step-by-step instructions and when we look at a sample reading.

Layout Versions
There are two versions of the layout—the original 8 x 4 + 4 and the 9 x 4.

8 x 4 +4

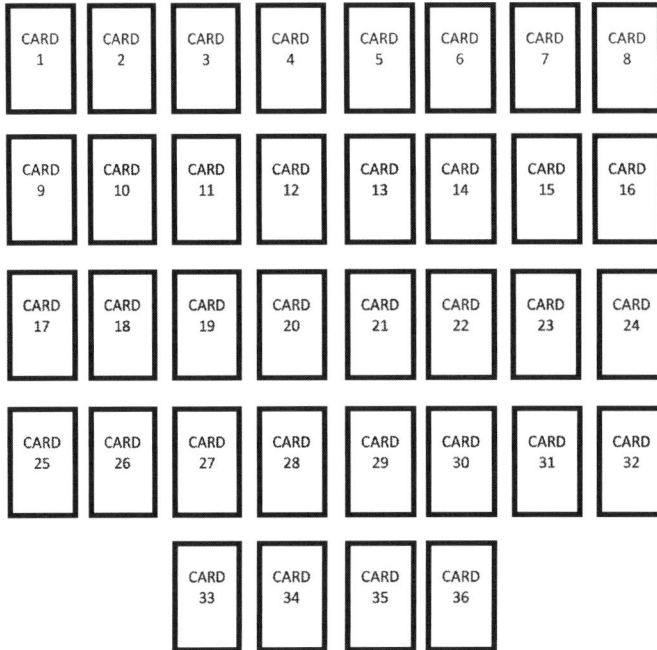

9 x 4

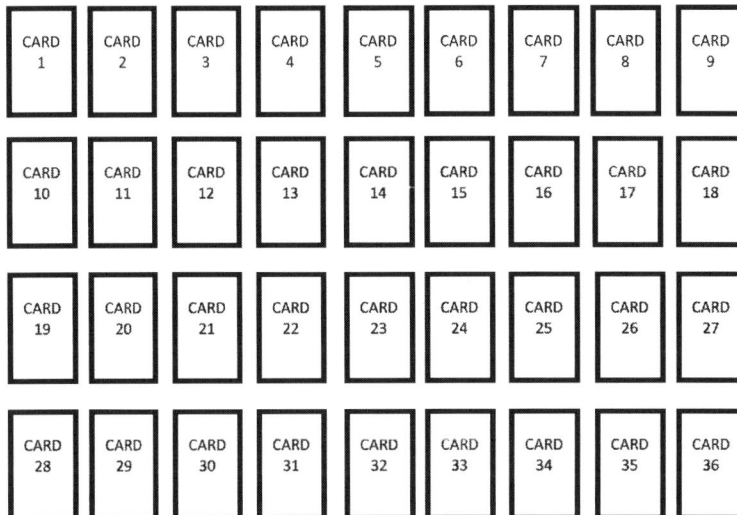

What's The Difference? Which is Best?

I personally tend to use the 9 x 4 but that's just me: either is fine. The same basic reading principles apply to both layouts. The difference is, the 8x 4 + 4 uses the bottom four cards as an overview of the reading, whereas the 9 x 4 will use the first four cards that way.

Again, decide which layout you're going to use as you shuffle and it'll be fine.

Other Features of The Grand Tableau

You will find as you go through the steps that the Grand Tableau incorporates some of the methods from other readings, particularly the 9 card spread. It is in this layout that a reader can also utilise a number of more advanced reading techniques, to add information:

Mirroring - where you pair with the cards' opposite numbers on each axis
Reflection - another type of mirroring, which gives you extra information
Knighting, where you look at cards in the knight position i.e. 2 cards along and then 1 either side from your querent or any other card you are interested in
Houses, where the *position* of each card represents a "House", which lends its energy to whatever card falls inside it.

MIRRORING AND REFLECTION

Mirroring is where you pair the card you're interested in with those in the opposite positions on the axis.

In the Grand Tableau Spread, Card 1 is mirrored by Cards 28 and 9, Card 2 by Cards 29 and 8, and so on. Note that the cards in the middle column are only mirrored by one card each, whereas it's two in all the other columns

So in the following example, whichever card is in position **12** (highlighted) is mirrored by Card 21 on the vertical and 16 on the horizontal. You would read them as Cards 12 +21, and 12+16.

CARD 1	CARD 2	CARD 3	CARD 4	CARD 5	CARD 6	CARD 7	CARD 8	CARD 9
CARD 10	CARD 11	CARD 12	CARD 13	CARD 14	CARD 15	CARD 16	CARD 17	CARD 18
CARD 19	CARD 20	CARD 21	CARD 22	CARD 23	CARD 24	CARD 25	CARD 26	CARD 27
CARD 28	CARD 29	CARD 30	CARD 31	CARD 32	CARD 33	CARD 34	CARD 35	CARD 36

Reflected cards on the other hand are those that appear in the *exactly* opposite position, as if you had folded the layout diagonally.

Card 1 is reflected by Card 36, Card 2 by Card 35 and so on, all the way through the 36 cards. Each card has only **one** reflected card. So in our Card 12 example again, Card 12 will always be reflected by Card 25. Again, you read them in pairs, so this would be the combination of Cards 12+25.

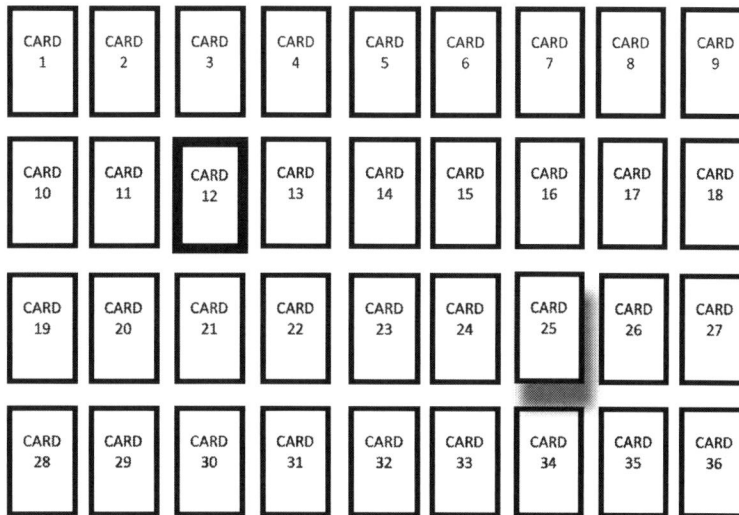

KNIGHTING

Knighting (as in, the chess term) is a bit more complicated. This position is 2 along and then 1 away from the card you are looking at.

So as you can see below, Card 12 is knighted by Cards 1,19, 29, 31, 5, 23.

I tend to read knighted cards in pairs along with my original card, using the knighting card to describe the one I am focusing on (so pairing Card 12 with Card 1, and so on.) You can also often get additional information by combining the knighting cards that are on the same axis together. So, here that would be Cards 1+19, 1+5, 19+23, 5+23, 29+31.

CARD 1	CARD 2	CARD 3	CARD 4	CARD 5	CARD 6	CARD 7	CARD 8	CARD 9
CARD 10	CARD 11	CARD 12	CARD 13	CARD 14	CARD 15	CARD 16	CARD 17	CARD 18
CARD 19	CARD 20	CARD 21	CARD 22	CARD 23	CARD 24	CARD 25	CARD 26	CARD 27
CARD 28	CARD 29	CARD 30	CARD 31	CARD 32	CARD 33	CARD 34	CARD 35	CARD 36

HOUSES

The Lenormand Houses reference the position of the cards on the Grand Tableau grid. Card 1, regardless of what the actual card is, is always in the House of the Rider, Card 2 in the House of the Clover and so on.

The meanings of the houses are the same as the meanings of the corresponding cards. So:

- ✤ The House of the **Rider** means visits, arrivals, news
- ✤The House of the **Clover**, luck and good fortune, chances
- ✤The House of the **Ship**, journeys and travel and so on

1 RIDER	2 CLOVER	3 SHIP	4 HOUSE	5 TREE	6 CLOUDS	7 SNAKE	8 COFFIN	9 BOUQUET
10 SCYTHE	11 WHIP	12 BIRDS	13 CHILD	14 FOX	15 BEAR	16 STARS	17 STORKS	18 DOG
19 TOWER	20 GARDEN	21 MOUNTAIN	22 CROSSROADS	23 MICE	24 HEART	25 RING	26 BOOK	27 LETTER
28 MAN	29 WOMAN	30 LILY	31 SUN	32 MOON	33 KEY	34 FISH	35 ANCHOR	36 CROSS

For example, *any* card that falls into **Position 1** can be read 'in the **House of the Rider'** i.e. in relation to visits and arrivals.

You read whichever card falls into that position alongside its house. Generally speaking, I would say that the card takes on the vibration of the House it falls in. So, for instance, imagine the card I had in my House 1, Rider position was, say, the **Garden**.

I have the **Garden**, meaning social life, public, groups appearing in my **Rider** house, meaning visits and arrivals.

So my Garden card in this position indicates a very busy social life with a lot of visitors. What if I had the **Anchor** card in the House of the Rider instead of the Garden? That would suggest "the long term" in the house of visits, news and arrivals. That probably indicates a long-stay visit of some kind, or that something new that turns up is set to stay.

House Meanings In The Grand Tableau

NEWS & VISITS	LUCK & CHANCE	TRAVEL & TRANS-PORT	HOME & FAMILY	HEALTH & VITALITY	HIDDEN, UNCLEAR AREAS	TROUBLE & PROBLEMS	ENDINGS	BLESSINGS
DECISIONS & CUTS	EFFORT & STRUGGLE	COMMS & TALKING	CHILDREN & YOUNG PEOPLE	WORK & SURVIVAL	FINANCES & POWER	GOALS, HOPES & DREAMS	NEW STARTS	FRIENDS & ALLIES
OFFICIALS & STATUS	SOCIAL LIFE & PUBLIC	BLOCKS & DELAYS	CHOICES & PATHS	WORRIES	LOVE	AGREE-MENTS & DEALS	KNOW-LEDGE & LEARNING	MESSAGES & DOC-UMENTS
A MAN	A WOMAN	AGE & WISDOM	SUCCESS & HAPPINESS	CREATIVE MATTERS & FEELINGS	FATE & SIGNIFI-CANCE	BUSINESS & FREEDOM	STABILITY	BURDENS

HOW TO READ THE GRAND TABLEAU

There is no single way to read the Grand Tableau. It is a *huge* reading with a lot of potential information available to you, and depending on your situation, you may not need all of it. Different readers have slightly different methods for reading, and you can be as detailed (or not) as you wish.

I'm going to give you the steps I use personally - I've found they work pretty well. In your own practice, I would try them out and pick and choose the ones you find most helpful.

Steps For Reading The Grand Tableau

Step 1
Shuffle and cut the cards using your normal method and lay all the cards out in a 9 x 4 grid or 8x4+4 as above

Step 2
To get a general idea of the themes of the entire reading look at **Cards 1-4** on your grid, and then the corner cards, reading them diagonally in pairs.

So in a 9 x 4 layout, you'll be reading cards **1 + 36**, cards **28 + 9**

In a **8 x 4 + 4** reading, take the **bottom 4 cards as your overview** instead, but use the corner cards as above

Step 3
Locate the **Querent** card. This will be the Woman for a female querent and the Man for a male querent. The position of this card is crucial as it affects the whole of the reading.

✤ Cards to the left of the Querent are generally read as past influences. Cards to the right are future influences. You can see from this position whether the querent is being heavily influenced by the past or not.

✤ Cards above the Querent are more conscious influences, and cards below, unconscious influences. You can see from this how "in control" of things the querent is at the current time. The higher up in the grid, the more control the querent has over events.

✤ Cards closest to the Querent obviously have the greatest influence at the present time.

✤ Also consider the **House position** (see details above) of the Querent card on the grid, as this gives a thematic clue. For example, if my querent is a woman, and she appears in position 14 on the grid, then she is appearing in the **House of the Fox**, i.e. work and employment, day to day survival but also deceptions. This indicates such issues are influencing her at the present time.

Step 4
Read the cards *immediately surrounding* the Querent in the same way as a 9-card spread, with the Querent at the centre. Obviously, this will depend on your Querent's position in the grid as a whole - you may only be able to do this partially.

Step 5
Read the cards in both the vertical and horizontal lines that the Querent appears in, as a chain reading, and reading the cards in pairs (you can also use Mirroring for this in the same ways as we do in the 5-card spread)

   ✤ For example, if our Querent is in position 14, we could read: Cards 5, Cards 23+24. Cards 10+11, Cards 12+ 13, Cards 15+16, Cards 17+18

   ✤ Also read the cards diagonally, which will move you from past influences to future ones.

Step 6

You can miss out this step if you like, and just move onto Step 7, but I find I prefer to have a detailed overview of the reading as a whole, especially if it's an annual or monthly reading. So I do tend to carry out this step.

- ❖ First, read ALL 4 horizontal rows, one after the other. For the quickest version, you can use mirroring and card combinations. So in Row 1, for example, you read Cards 1+9, Card 2+8, Cards 3+7, Cards 4+6, Card 5.
- ❖ For more detail, you can read across the row in pairs - Cards 1+2, 2+3, 3+4 etc, remembering that you are moving from past influences towards future ones
- ❖ Then, read ALL 9 vertical rows, one after the other. Again, for the quickest version, you can use mirroring and card combinations. So in Column 1, for example, you read Cards 1+28, 10+19. For more detail, read down the columns in pairs e.g. Cards 1+10, 19+28

Step 7

Note the positions of any particular key cards representing the different life areas, especially those the Querent is interested in. For example, the Heart for love life, Bear for money, the other Man or Woman card (or Dog) for partners, and so on. This will depend really on matters of interest for the Querent.

- ❖ Bear in mind these key cards' positions in the reading - I'm usually more interested in things coming up than what's in the past but it is dependent on the situation. You can explore any aspect of the querent's life you want to, and get lots of information.
- ❖ You can use reading techniques like the 9-card spread around these key cards if you want to explore further.

Step 8

For any cards or areas you are interested in exploring further, you can also note the **House** position, and the cards **Mirroring, Reflecting and Knighting** it. You can even do this for every single card in the reading. Be aware, that this is not a quick task, but does yield very interesting information & hidden tidbits. To do so, for each card   I would read:

- ❧ The card in its House, with the card being given the vibration of its house
- ❧ Each Mirrored card and the Reflected card in a pair with the card in question
- ❧ Each Knight card in combination with the card in question and then all knighting cards from the same axis in paired combinations

EXAMPLE READING

Q: What is coming up for me in the next few months?

1 RIDER	13 CHILD	30 LILY	20 GARDEN	8 COFFIN	35 ANCHOR	32 MOON	31 SUN	27 LETTER
26 BOOK	28 MAN	15 BEAR	19 TOWER	11 WHIP	29 WOMAN	4 HOUSE	18 DOG	22 CROSSROADS
23 MICE	5 TREE	10 SCYTHE	16 STARS	24 HEART	17 STORKS	3 SHIP	12 BIRDS	33 KEY
7 SNAKE	21 MOUNTAIN	36 CROSS	9 BOUQUET	14 FOX	34 FISH	25 RING	6 CLOUDS	2 CLOVER

I'm going to through every step with this, so I warn you, it's not going to be a quick read. However, it will help you to see the Grand Tableau in action.

Step 1

I shuffle and lay out the grid in a 9x4 formation, as above.

Step 2

I look at the themes of the entire reading:

Cards 1-4:

Rider—Child—Lily—Garden = An upcoming group or a gathering for mature beginners or older children

Corner cards:

Rider—Clover = Luck/Good fortune arrives
Snake—Letter = Written or documented problem/bad news

Step 3

The Querent card is the **Woman**. She is appearing in the second row in **House 15 Bear**, which is around Money and Power. We can see from her position in the grid that there are a lot of influences passing, most of the negative cards are in the past, and although there's some difficulty near her there's a general positivity about the cards coming up.

Step 4

The cards immediately surrounding the Querent are as follows, so we can read them like a 9-card spread.

Coffin—Anchor—Moon
Whip—Woman—House
Heart—Storks—Ship

Reading the diamond anti-clockwise round the Woman —**Anchor-Whip, Whip-Storks, Storks-House, House-Anchor** to get the overall picture of what surrounds her, we see:

❖ A constant struggle, a tough new start, new living arrangements or a house move, a stable home
❖ Then, on her mind is a drawn out ending and emotional/creative stability (**Coffin-Anchor-Moon**)
❖ At the moment, she seems to be having a hard time at home, or pushing herself hard (**Whip-Woman-House**)
❖ There's also extra information about a new love or passion and the start of a new journey (**Heart-Storks-Ship**)
❖ Moving out of the situation is a difficult ending of some type, possibly the end of a love or sexual relationship or just passionate hard work (**Coffin-Whip-Heart**)
❖ Currently, she has a sense of a stable new start, a permanent change (**Anchor-Woman-Storks**)
❖ Coming into the picture is perhaps emotions about home, and possibly moving around or living somewhere temporarily (**Moon-House-Ship**)
❖ Perhaps a journey is coming to an end, or a new one is being embarked on after an ending (**Coffin-Woman-Ship**)
❖There's also an indication of either a love affair or creative passions (**Heart-Woman-Moon**)

Step 5

So now I'll read the vertical and horizontal lines that our Querent appears in ONLY.

First, the vertical:

The Querent has stability on her mind (the **Anchor** right above her), and we see from the cards below her (**Storks-Fish**) that this is about a new or start-up business or career.

Then, the horizontal:

With regard to the money/power situation that's behind this, it looks as if there's either a powerful, protective man or manager (**Man-Bear**), the bank, possibly or someone with high status power (**Bear-Tower**) who's been giving her a hard time or training her in some way (**Tower-Whip**). It could be a writer or publisher though (**Book-Man**) or an accountant.

Coming up ahead of her is a friend's house or domain (**House-Dog**) and a choice of some sort - or perhaps several friends (**Dog-Crossroads**).

And the diagonal, with a bit more detail around the cards appearing there:

As well as creativity also coming up for her (**Moon**), it looks as though she has an uncertain journey ahead and won't necessarily know how things are going to pan out (**Ship-Clouds**). Perhaps she should just go with the flow, as that uncertainty is followed by good luck (**Clover**). There also seems to be a significant conversation (**Birds-Key**) coming up connected with this journey (**Ship-Birds**), and it looks like a very lucky one (**Birds-Clover**). It also looks like it might be a significant turning point of some sort, a great twist of fate (**Key-Clover**).

Step 6. (Optional)

This depends whether or not you want more of an overview of the whole reading, or you just want to focus on specific areas. If you just want to focus on specific areas, go straight to Step 7.

Read all 4 Horizontal Rows

Row 1: Mirroring: News arrives **(Rider-Letter)**; successful young person or beginner **(Child-Sun)**; emotional/creative maturity **(Lily-Moon)**; stable social life **(Garden-Anchor), an ending (Coffin).**

As a chain: A young visitor or news about a young person or beginner; a maturing beginner; social or public maturity; social life ending; drawn out ending; emotional or creative stability; happy feelings or successful creative project; written success.

Row 2: As this is the Querent's Row, we have already covered the chain details of it above, but mirroring gives us: Multiple learnings, knowledge options or choice of book **(Book-Crossroads)**; a friendly or supportive male **(Man-Dog)**; domestic finances or power in her domain **(Bear-House)**; the woman's establishment, status or arrogance **(Tower-Woman)**, hard work, effort or a challenge **(Whip)**.

Row 3: Mirroring: Significant worries **(Mice-Key)**; communication health or growth **(Tree-Birds)**; travel decision or journey curtailed **(Scythe-Ship)**; a new ambition or hopes **(Stars-Storks)**; love or passion (Heart).

Chain: health, vitality or growth worries; curtailed health or development; ambition decision or hopes dashed; passionate ambition; a new passion; start of a new journey; communication trip or overseas; significant conversation.

Row 4: Mirroring: Lucky problem, silver lining **(Snake-Clover)**; unknown, hidden or unclear obstacle **(Mountain-Clouds)**; burdensome commitment or promise **(Cross-Ring)**; business or independence blessing **(Bouquet-Fish)**; work or survival **(Fox)**.

Chain: Blocked or delay problem; heavy or troublesome obstacle; pleasant burden or obligation; work blessing; freelance work; contracted business; unclear agreement; lucky or positive lack of clarity - just go with the flow.

Read All 9 Vertical Rows

Remember as we go along that these move us from the recent past into the future, and this depends on the position of the Querent.

Column 1: A problem's arisen (**Rider-Snake**). Anxious knowledge, learning or book (**Book-Mice**). Book news or knowledge arrives; anxious knowledge or learning; undermining or betrayal worries.

Column 2: Blocked young person or beginner (**Child-Mountain**); energetic, or karmically-linked male (**Man-Tree**). Male young person or beginner; energetic male; blocked growth.

Column 3: Burdened or troubled maturity or later years (**Lily-Cross**); reduced power, protection or finances (**Bear-Scythe**). Financial maturity or secure later years; reduced finances or protection; weighty decision.

Column 4: Lovely or blessed social life (**Garden-Bouquet**); ambitious or star status (**Tower-Stars**). High status or established group or social life; ambitious or status status; lovely or blessed ambitions and "stars"

Column 5: Work or job ending (**Coffin-Fox**); passions or loves are tested & get a work-out (**Whip-Heart**). Tough ending; passions or loves are tested; work passions.

Column 6: This is the Querent's column (the present time) so we've already covered this above, but in a nutshell: Business or freelance stability (**Anchor-Fish**); fresh start for the Querent (**Woman-Storks**).

Column 7: Promised creative project (**Moon-Ring**); travelling or mobile domain or 'home' (**House-Ship**); domain creativity or home feelings; travelling, temporary or moving domain; agreed journey or move.

Column 8: Unclear success (**Sun-Clouds**); communicative friends, advisors, Twitter friends (**Dog-Birds**). Friends' success; communicative, chatty friends; confused conversations or messages.

Column 9: Lucky letter, document or fortunate news (**Letter-Clover**); significant turning point (**Crossroad-Key**). Multiple documents, messages or writings; significant turning point; lucky destiny or fate.

Step 7
Houses - General
I tend to find this information most useful combined with the Knighting, Mirroring & Reflection as seen in Step 9, below. However, for an overview of the whole spread, it's worth noting all the cards' Houses.

Remember, the card that falls in a given house is given the vibration of that house, so here we have:

Card	House	
Card	*House*	
Rider	**Rider**	Visits and news. New things.
Child	**Clover**	New starts, children or young people have lucky influences
Lily	**Ship**	Older people travelling or experience overseas. Ageing progress.
Garden	**House**	Socialising at home; sociable and people-filled home-life
Coffin	**Tree**	Health problems; karmic endings
Anchor	**Clouds**	An uncertainty about the long term picture; lack of permanence
Moon	**Snake**	Emotional/ideals problems & upsets. Untrustworthy feelings.

Sun	**Coffin**	Successes may be marred
Letter	**Bouquet**	Gifts; positive news; news that brings happiness
Book	**Scythe**	Discovery; secret uncovered; book decision
Man	**Whip**	Arguments or conflict connected with a man or men
Bear	**Birds**	Money conversations; communication-related money
Tower	**Child**	Starter organisations, legal child; arrogant young people
Whip	**Fox**	Hard work; tough job; work training ; bruised by deception
Woman	**Bear**	Protected woman, well-off woman or sense of security
House	**Stars**	Domestic or personal ambitions, hopes, and dreams
Dog	**Storks**	New friendships, new starts & changes with friends
Crossroads	**Dog**	A lot of different friends; choices with friends
Mice	**Tower**	Structural or building problems; status being reduced
Tree	**Garden**	Healthy or flourishing social life or growing networks
Scythe	**Mountain**	Blocked decisions; brief delays
Stars	**Crossroads**	Multiple ambitions; hopes and dreams; pathways to goals
Heart	**Mice**	Love or passion worries; deeply felt or core anxieties
Storks	**Heart**	New start in love; beginnings of a new passion; change of heart
Ship	**Ring**	Travel or journey agreement or arrangement
Birds	**Book**	Discussing secrets or knowledge. Intellectual discussion
Key	**Letter**	Important document, significant news or message
Snake	**Man**	Difficult man; untrustworthy man, problems with a man
Mountain	**Woman**	Blocks and isolation for a woman
Cross	**Lily**	The burdens of experience and ageing. Troubled elders.
Bouquet	**Sun**	Lovely success; gifted success; prizes and gifts; positivity
Fox	**Moon**	Deceptive fantasies; creative or emotional work
Fish	**Key**	Significant business or freedom. Fated business. Key cashflow.
Ring	**Fish**	Business contracts, promises and agreements.
Clouds	**Anchor**	Insecurity; uncertainty over stability, lasting uncertainty
Clover	**Cross**	Luck comes with burdens and responsibilities

Step 8

Now let's pick specific cards and life areas to get more detail on. In this case, I'd like more information about: The **Coffin** card, so I can get some clarity about the ending we're discussing. The **Ship** card to understand what the querent's "journey" is about. The querent's new business with the **Fish** card. The significant bit of luck (**Clover/Key**) coming up.

Again, I have a choice here about how deep to go. I can do 9-card spreads using each of these as the keycard to drill down and get more detail. I can also use the Houses combined with the Knighting, Mirroring and Reflection techniques to find out more, which is what I've chosen to do below, so you can see it in action.

Step 9
Houses, Knighting, Mirroring, Reflection

❖ My Querent herself appears in the House of the Bear (**Finances, Protection**) showing that this is a key area for her, and is being knighted by the following: her sociability (**Garden**) and hopes and dreams (**Stars**), indicating she's ambitious as well as positive (**Sun**) and chatty (**Birds**). It shows her working, or a work persona (**Fox**) and that she's committed in some way (**Ring.**) Paired with each other, her knighted cards show an ambitious network or group (**Garden+Stars**), communication success (**Sun + Birds**) and possibly contracted or relationship-related work (**Fox + Ring**).

❖ Mirroring her is her status or officialdom (**Tower**) and a new start for her (**Storks**).

❖ The card reflecting her is the **Scythe** - so a decision of hers or possibly a reduction. Has she downsized?

❖ That ending - **Coffin** - appears in the House of the Tree (**Health/Energy & Karma**) so she'll need to watch her health and energy levels. It suggests she's very drained. The ending is being knighted as follows. Financial dreams (**Bear + Stars**) and a house move (**Storks House**). I think she's had to give up some of her dreams around having money for a house. It's being mirrored and reflected by the job card (**Fox**), so a job ending has put paid to all this for now.

♣ Now let's look at the **Ship** card to find out more about the journey ahead. It appears in the **House of the Ring**, which shows it is something agreed, pre-arranged or promised. It is being knighted by a previous tough time at work (**Whip-Fox**), need for stability (**Anchor**), success (**Sun**) and making lucky choices (**Crossroads-Clover**) in future. It's being mirrored by the living situation (**House**) and a past decision about that (**Scythe**). My guess is that she's not settled anywhere permanently yet and things are in flux. Her finances are also fluctuating as shown by the reflection of the **Bear** card. Either that or there's money transferring or money from abroad.

♣ The **Fish** card appears in the **House of the Key** (Fate or Importance) and it's showing her business or freedom being knighted by ambition and hard work (**Stars-Whip**). It is home-based (**House**) and involves some sort of communication or social media (**Birds**). It is being mirrored by something possibly artistic or design-related (**Bouquet**) or simply pleasant as well as long-term. (**Anchor**). There is a social or public element to the business, that is showing in the reflecting card (**Garden**)

♣ The luck (**Clover**) appears in the House of the Cross (**Responsibilities & Burdens**) so either does not come without a price, or has arisen from a pressured situation. It is being knighted by the journey (**Ship**) and also a friend or companion (**Dog**). It seems to spring from a problem as seen by the mirrored cards (**Snake**) with a document (**Letter**) or perhaps some bad news. This bit of luck is being reflected by the Rider card so it's definitely on its way.

So there we have it. A detailed general reading using the Grand Tableau! Can you see now why it's not a reading that you'd do on a daily basis? As its name suggest, it's really for the Big Picture stuff.

Also, you don't need ALL the detail. Check the chart overleaf to decide how much detail you want for your particular purposes and what techniques to use in each case.

What I Want	Grand Tableau Techniques
A very broad overview e.g for coming month	• 4 corners, 1st 4 cards • 9 card spread around querent card • Horizontal and verticals around querent • Mirrored card readings of all rows & columns.
A general reading with focus just on specific areas e.g. for coming three to six months looking at love, health, career etc as required	• 4 corners, 1st 4 cards • 9 card spread around querent card • Horizontals, verticals, diagonals around querent • Mirrored card readings of all rows & columns, plus chained for more detail • 9 card spread around any area of interest e.g Bear for money, Heart for love
A detailed general reading with additional information on any area of interest e.g for coming year	• 4 corners, 1st 4 cards • 9 card spread around querent card • Horizontals, verticals, diagonals around querent • Mirrored card readings of all rows & columns, plus chained for more detail • 9 card spread around any area of interest e.g Bear for money, Heart for love • House positions • Knighting, mirroring, reflection for any areas of interest
A detailed reading which includes every possible area of life e.g for coming year to three years	• 4 corners, 1st 4 cards • 9 card spread around querent card • Horizontals, verticals, diagonals around querent • Mirrored card readings of all rows & columns, plus chained for more detail • 9 card spread for ALL main areas of life e.g Bear for money, Heart for love, Tree for Health, Snake for problems etc • House positions for all 36 cards, combined with knighting, mirroring, reflection for each card, one by one.

III

LENORMAND IN PRACTICE

WORKING WITH LENORMAND CARDS IN PRACTICE

Now we've covered the very basics & layout-reading steps, I want to get more into the nitty-gritty of Lenormand, and look both at how you might develop your own regular practice as well as ways you can deepen both your understanding of the card meanings and the Lenormand system for greater accuracy in your readings.

As you develop as a Lenormand reader, it's important that you start to build a degree of independence and confidence with both the card meanings and your readings. In this section, we'll be going through some of the key issues to think about, as well as answering some of the main questions I hear from beginning readers. Again, I'm including various tasks and exercises for you where necessary, to help you on your journey!

In order for you to develop as a Lenormand reader, you need to build the following:

❖ An intuitive knowledge of the basic card meanings & how they apply in different contexts
❖ An understanding of how card combinations work
❖ A knowledge of how to ask the best questions to get the answers you want
❖ The ability to link card combinations into a story in each of the layouts
❖ A regular practice and your own relationship with the cards

Understanding Card Meanings & Context

You'll note that in the **Card Meaning** pages I gave you examples of the card meanings from different contexts including Love & Relationships, Career & Business and for describing People.

"But why so many meanings? " I hear you cry. "How am I supposed to know which is the right one? How on earth can I learn them all?"

This can be really difficult to grasp when you're first starting to read the cards. But the key to unlocking the Lenormand is not to learn the meanings by rote, as if you are in school, but to understand the core universal meanings that lie underneath and then learn to *apply* those meanings to the different situations and contexts in your everyday world. The context is just as important when it comes to Lenormand readings as the underlying card meanings and how they combine. If Lenormand is a language of symbols that you use to tell a story, the context is that story's setting, or its story *type*, its genre. If someone's asking you a question about their career, you don't want to start going on about the ins and outs of their love life. Likewise, if someone's asked you about their love life, you're not going to answer them by talking about their finances.

The truth is that the cards' meanings exist and deepen in relation to one another and the world around us. Lenormand, as I have said, is a storytelling system, which uses fundamental human meanings and concepts represented by the cards: things like, truth (**Key**), betrayal (**Snake**), love (**Heart**), protection (**Bear**), survival (**Fox**), youth (**Child**), ageing (**Lily**), conflict (**Whip**), and combines them together to create narratives or stories that make sense.

This is why the lists of meanings I and other readers provide can never include every possible meaning. They are intended only as guidance and examples of *how* those underlying concepts manifest out in the everyday world. In many ways, the time period and country you live in doesn't matter. Yes, the decks themselves often have very Euro-centric artwork & 18th century imagery because that's where and when they originated, but you can still apply those universal meanings to whatever culture, world or situation you're living in: it's one of the reasons Lenormand has lasted a long time.

Let me show you what I mean, by taking a look at just one card, its underlying meaning, and how that might manifest out in the world today, in multiple different contexts.

Lenormand Meaning Example: The SHIP

Take your Lenormand **Ship** card, or simply picture a ship, any ship. Maybe a galleon, of the kind often portrayed in the Lenormand cards, but it could be a yacht, a ferry, a cruise ship, any kind of ship.

Now, do as I suggested previously, and try to think of as many uses or features of a ship as you possibly can.

When I think of a Ship, I primarily think of overseas travel, of going far away. I think of holidays. I think of transport and going from Place A to Place B. I think of imports and exports and trade, of immigration and emigration, of exploration and adventure and the bringing of goods and people from one place to another, all over the world.

Now when I think about all this, I also get a sort of underlying sense of what connects them all. Do you? Can you feel it?

If I had to put that entire sense into just one phrase, I would personally say it's something like:

Movement from A to B

That is the underlying meaning of the Ship card. And that is the meaning we can now apply to specific different situations in our everyday lives and in our readings.

So let's now take a closer look when those meanings are applied in different contexts.

Ways that an underlying concept of *Movement from A to B* might manifest…

In day-to-day life: Transport, travel, trains, cars, buses, trips, holidays

In a business: Transfers, shipping, freight

As an activity: Travel and exploration, going on a journey of any type

At home: Moving house

In love: A romantic trip, a person from overseas

Psychologically: A metaphorical journey of development

In a person: A traveller, someone always on the move or with broad horizons

In a career: Career movement, travel for your job, overseas work, transfers

See how it works? The card has one underlying meaning, but you can apply that underlying meaning to multiple situations and contexts. You can apply it to pretty much any situation you want and come up with a meaning AS LONG AS the meaning derives from that underlying concept.

That is why card meaning lists may seem to have so many different meanings for one card. They are manifestations of the **underlying** concept or essence. The lists are designed to be useful guides and quick references, so usually the examples you will see are the most common ones.

Developing a strong sense of that underlying meaning also helps when you are trying to differentiate between two cards which might in some ways seem similar. The nuances are often extremely significant when it comes to doing Lenormand readings and understanding what the cards are saying accurately.

For example, let's take the **Ship** and the **Garden** cards. Both cards have a sense of "out in the world" about them. But whereas the Ship is focused on the *movement*, the Place A & Place B side of the world, the Garden focuses more on the *public and the collective*, the people, the social world.

Now take another look at the Ship Card meanings and combinations at the front of the book. Do they make a bit more sense now? Can you see how I have arrived at them and they are not random or arbitrary?

At the end of the book, you'll find some practice readings you can try in different contexts.

How To Get More Confident With Card Meanings

To be able to use Lenormand most effectively and confidently, you have to start building an intuitive relationship with your cards. A lot of this is to do with having an instinctive understanding of the underlying meanings of their symbols, as in the Ship example above. The tips below are some ideas as to how you can start to do that.

Move Away From The Lists!

The card meaning lists that Lenormand readers like myself provide are meant to help and support you. They are often examples of how the underlying meanings of the cards manifest in day to day life; they are not absolute and they don't include all possible interpretations, just the main ones usually.   Getting confused about multiple meanings is usually because you're relying too heavily on these *external* interpretations and examples rather than thinking about what connects them: the underlying meaning of the symbol itself.

To start to get to grips with the card meanings in a more intuitive way, you need to put the lists away. They are most useful as a reference or to check back, but focusing on the cards and symbols for yourself will take you into their meanings more deeply in the long run and yield richer results.

Get To Know Your Cards

A Lenormand journal is a great place to start doing this. You can do it over a period of time, but, you'll need to get to know each individual card and its symbol in depth, one by one.

 First of all, think about the object, person or animal shown the card. Think about it in the real world. What is it used for? How many uses can you think of? If it is an animal or person, how does it behave and look? What is it known for? Does this symbol have any particular cultural meanings? Does the word for the symbol have meanings in your language?

Make notes about anything and everything you can. For example, here are some possible notes about the **Key** symbol. Remember, I am thinking about a key, any key, in terms of real day to day life: both practically and how the symbol and sometimes word gets used in the culture around me.

A KEY:
♣ Opens the door or a box of treasure!

✤ Unlocks something important or valuable
✤ Means "the answer" or "the final clue" to a puzzle or mystery
✤ Often has a connection with magic in some way
✤ Can be very ornate, shows its importance
✤ In English, we use the word "key" to mean "most important" e.g. "Key points" "Key player" etc.

Try to note as many things as you can. DON'T consult any Lenormand card meaning lists; just think about the object, person or animal itself, as it is.

Consider The Symbol's Underlying Meanings

Once you've thought of all the things you can, you are probably starting to get a sense, a kind of inner feeling about what connects them, what that symbol means at a deeper level. Sometimes this is hard to articulate or put into words; it's more something conceptual that you just feel and "know". If you can, see if you can jot down a few words that represent and connect this underlying meaning or concept. So, for example, for Key, I might put: Important, Significant. THE one answer. THE most important thing.

Think About How Those Underlying Meanings Manifest In Everyday Life

So that concept or idea - how does it show up in our day to day lives and in different circumstances & contexts? It can manifest in multiple ways.

Jot down some notes about this for the symbol you are focusing on. In the case of a key, the concept of important, significant, THE one, THE most important could manifest as:

In General

The physical object: an actual key

Something or someone highly important or the most important

An answer, the answer, to a question

Fate, something destined to happen

Significant events

In Love

The one, a soulmate

Romantic destiny or fate

At Work

An important idea

The solution to a problem

A significant person

Money

The one single thing that will bring you money; the key to your financial situation

Practice!

Do as many readings for yourself as you can. Keep a record, both of the readings and results and note any patterns, particularly with card meanings and how they tend to show up in your life. You will often find that some variants of the cards' meanings don't show up for you at all, whereas others do often.

I am like this, as are a lot of readers, with regard to the Lily card. Some lists of interpretations have sex as one of the main Lily meanings. I can see why; the opening and closing shape of the flower, the flower's protruding stamen, the fact it's heavily scented and sensual. In fact, the so-called German "school" of Lenormand meanings usually has sex as one of the meanings of Lily. But I have never used this card to represent sex personally although feel free to; I tend, like many readers, to use the Whip instead and the Bouquet for pleasure and beauty.

For the Lily, I tend to use the meanings related to maturity, age, experience, wisdom and peace. I do not personally agonise about whether or not it might mean "sex" in my situation just because it does for some other readers and they relate to it that way. For me, it just tends not to. And my readings and interpretations, since it is me that's doing them, will tend to reflect that.

Exercise I
Getting To Know Card Meanings Intuitively

Here's a practice exercise to help you gain more confidence in understanding Lenormand card meanings, for three cards of your choosing.

The exercise is about getting to know the Lenormand Card Meanings better through understanding the **universal and underlying symbols** they represent.
It is **not** about checking the lists or learning by rote, or the "correct" answer. It's about using your intuition and knowledge. Because this is about you and your relationship with your cards, you should try not to refer to Lenormand Card Meaning lists at ANY point while you are making notes.

The Task:

• First, pick a card at random from your Lenormand deck.

• Think about the object, animal or thing depicted in the card and how it appears in **real life** & culture. Make notes overleaf about that symbol—just jot down anything you want, as quickly as you can. Words, phrases, ideas; anything you can think of. If the symbol is an **object or place**, what is the object or place for in life? What does it do? What are some of its key features? How do people use it? If the symbol is a **figure or an animal,** what are its physical features? How does it generally behave? What is it known for? Is the word for that symbol used in everyday life? What for?

• Now think about the underlying meaning or "feel" of all those things, what it is that connects them. Can you note just two or three words that capture that essence or underlying meaning?

• How would you apply **that** meaning to:

   Love & relationships?
   Career & Work?
   Your own life in general?

Now repeat the exercise for two more cards

Remember, do **NOT** check Lenormand Card Meaning lists at all while you're doing this exercise; wait until you've finished with the three cards you pick. The results may surprise you; you may well find you know more than you realise!

1. Card _____

This Object, Animal, Figure in Real Life

_____

_____

_____

_____

Underlying meaning? (Two or three words only)

_____

Examples of **this** underlying meaning as it might apply:

In work or career

_____

In relationships or for a person

_____

In your own daily life as it is at the moment

_____

2. Card   _____

This Object, Animal, Figure in Real Life

_____

_____

_____

_____

Underlying meaning? (Two or three words only)

_____

Examples of **this** underlying meaning as it might apply:

In work or career

_____

In relationships or for a person

_____

In your own daily life as it is at the moment

_____

3. Card   _____

This Object, Animal, Figure in Real Life

_____

_____

_____

_____

Underlying meaning? (Two or three words only)

_____

Examples of **this** underlying meaning as it might apply:

In work or career

_____

In relationships or for a person

_____

In your own daily life as it is at the moment

_____

Over time, if you are keeping a Lenormand journal, you can build up a personal "dossier" of all 36 cards cards in this way. If you want to check how well these relate to the "real" meanings, now take a look back at the detailed meanings for your cards listed at the start of the book.

Exercise II
Test Yourself On Card Meanings

Use the exercises in this section to help test your knowledge and understanding of the cards. It's best to try and fill them in yourself if you can without referring back. The aim of them is to help build your confidence and independence in reading the cards, and help prise you from reliance on card meaning and card combination lists!

Answers are provided on p.

1: Nouns: Things, People, Concepts
Which cards might you associate with the following?

Attractiveness   _____

New Start   _____

Burdens   _____

Uncertainty   _____

Marriage   _____

Emotion   _____

Trouble   _____

Breakup   _____

Papers   _____

Business   _____

Ambition   _____

Family   _____

Friendship   _____

Officialdom   _____

Education   _____

Success   _____

Good Fortune   _____

Delays   _____

Young Person   _____

Social Life   _____

Conversation   _____

Stability   _____

Conflict   _____

Travel   _____

Ending   _____

Visitor   _____

2: Adjectives, Modifiers, Descriptors

And the following?

Mature   _____

Verbal   _____

Anxious   _____

Written   _____

Celebrity   _____

Happy   _____

Public   _____

Important   _____

Financial   _____

Corporate   _____

Negative   _____

Committed   _____

Lovely   _____

Harsh   _____

Karmic   _____

Fresh   _____

Healthy   _____

Secure   _____

Masculine   _____

Naive   _____

Moody   _____

Secret   _____

Domestic   _____

Isolated   _____

Arrogant   _____

Confusing   _____

Friendly   _____

3: Nouns, Things, People II

Which nouns—things, people etc—might you link with   the following cards?

Fish   _____

Whip   _____

Clouds   _____

Crossroads   _____

Storks   _____

Scythe   _____

Coffin   _____

Bouquet   _____

Tower   _____

Stars   _____

Book   _____

House   _____

Garden   _____

Dog   _____

Ship   _____

Sun   _____

Tree   _____

Mountain   _____

Cross   _____

Heart   _____

Ring   _____

Birds   _____

Lily   _____

Moon   _____

Rider   _____

Anchor   _____

Fox   _____

4: Adjectives, Modifiers, Descriptors II

Which adjectives might you link with these cards?

Snake   _____

Lily   _____

Child   _____

Scythe   _____

Bouquet   _____

Tree   _____

Heart   _____

Key   _____

Fox   _____

Mice   _____

Book   _____

Cross   _____

Ship   _____

Moon   _____

Fish   _____

Clover   _____

Rider   _____

Anchor   _____

Tower   _____

House   _____

Bear   _____

Ring   _____

Mountain   _____

Garden   _____

Birds   _____

Letter   _____

You can check your answers on **p. 288**.

Understanding Card Combinations

To 'get' card combinations, the most important thing is to know how the cards work together in pairs.

As a reminder, the *first* card in the pair can be read as a **Noun**—a thing, a person, a name The *second* card in the pair can be read as an **Adjective**—the description or modification of that thing or person

e.g. **Ring + Mice** = Relationship (Noun) + Anxious (Adjective)
= Anxious Relationship

Man + Bouquet = Man (Noun) + Good-Looking (Bouquet)
= Good-Looking Man

BUT you need to remember that all the cards can have more than one meaning - which means that all the Combinations can also have multiple possible meanings.

Let's look at the Ring + Mice example again with just some of the meanings each of those cards can have:

RING Meanings (Nouns)	MICE Meanings (Adjectives)
Relationship	Anxious
Agreement	Worried
Contract	Concerning
Deal	Panicky
Marriage	Distressed
Payment	Nervous
Bond	Frightened

If I combine all of those, I get lots of potential meanings—**49** possible combinations just from the above two lists alone! Some of which will have identical meanings, some which won't, and some which make more sense than others.

For example:
Anxious Relationship = a relationship filled with anxiety
Concerning Marriage = a marriage that worries others
Panicked Deal = Perhaps a deal that has been struck out of fear? That someone has rushed into?
Frightened or Anxious Bond = Some kind of link or agreement made under duress?

This is why the **context** of your reading is so very important.

If you are talking to a Mafia Boss (OK, highly unlikely, I agree!) an agreement made under duress might make sense. A lovestruck teen worrying about their first relationship? A different matter entirely. Someone struggling with their finances could well have been in a total panic and signed up unwisely for a loan they're now going to be held to.

ALWAYS consider the context of your reading, as well as the things you already know about the person you're reading for and the question. It's the key to your readings and whether or not they're going to make sense.

It's also the reason it's important to try to develop the ability to read combinations more organically for yourself, rather than relying all the time on other people's lists. Card Combination lists are provided as useful guides, that's all. By using them, you can see the most common meanings and those that particular readers have come up with. They are great back-ups to have, to find interpretations you might not have thought of—but rather like a young person gaining independence, it's important to try to free yourself from over-reliance on them.

Exercise III
Making Card Combinations

This exercise is designed to help you practice card combinations

The Task:

- Pick two cards at random from your deck & note them below.

- For the first card, list as many meanings as you can in NOUN form. For the second card, list as many meanings as you can in ADJECTIVE form.

- Finally, list as many meanings as you can for that COMBINATION.

Card 1	Card 2
_____	_____
Meanings (Noun)	**Meanings (Adj.)**
_____	_____
_____	_____
_____	_____
_____	_____
_____	_____
_____	_____

Card Combinations

_____

_____

_____

_____

_____

_____

_____

Now, repeat the exercise for a different randomly-drawn pair of cards.

Card 1	Card 2
_____	_____
Meanings (Noun)	**Meanings (Adj.)**
_____	_____
_____	_____
_____	_____
_____	_____
_____	_____
_____	_____

Card Combinations

_____

_____

_____

_____

_____

_____

_____

Now check against the card combinations at the start of the book. Can you better see where they are coming from? How do they compare with yours?

Exercise IV
Test Yourself On Card Combinations

Without looking them up in the card combination lists, now try testing yourself on these combinations

What could these combinations mean?

Man + Scythe   _____

Fox + Anchor   _____

Ring + Sun   _____

Woman + Bouquet   _____

Snake + Scythe   _____

Bear + Clover   _____

Tree + Cross   _____

Book + Key   _____

Key + Woman   _____

Stars + Ship   _____

Which pairs of cards could represent these?

A Marriage Ending   _____

Lovely options   _____

Health worries   _____

Friendly advice   _____

A difficult job   _____

Secret affair   _____

Celebrity artist   _____

Therapy   _____

Financial luck   _____

Business meeting   _____

Sexy woman   _____

Travel delays   _____

Arrogant man   _____

Great happiness   _____

You can check your answers on **p. 292.**

Exercise V
Card Combinations In Context

Now, to take it a step further, here's an exercise to help you practice applying card meanings and combinations to different contexts.

In this task, we'll be picking two random cards and applying their meanings to different contexts.

The Task:

- Choose two cards at random from your Lenormand deck

- For both cards separately, list as many meanings as you can for the contexts given.

- Using the Noun+Adjective card combination method, combine your two cards in as many ways as you can for the contexts given.

Card 1

_____

Basic Meaning: _____

In The Context Of…

Everyday Life _____

In A Business   _____

As An Activity   _____

In Technology   _____

At Home   _____

In Love   _____

In Health   _____

Psychologically   _____

In A Friendship   _____

In A Job   _____

In A Person   _____

Card 2

_____

Basic Meaning: _____

In The Context Of…

Everyday Life   _____

In A Business   _____

As An Activity   _____

In Technology   _____

At Home   _____

In Love   _____

In Health   _____

Psychologically   _____

In A Friendship   _____

In A Job   _____

In A Person   _____

How do these compare to the contextual meanings at the start of the book in the Card Meanings section?

Cards 1 + 2

_____ + _____

Basic Combo Meaning: _____

In The Context Of…

Everyday Life _____

In A Business _____

As An Activity _____

In Technology _____

At Home _____

In Love _____

In Health _____

Psychologically _____

In A Friendship _____

In A Job _____

In A Person _____

Now check the relevant combinations at the start of the book. Can you see how these could be applied and change according to different contexts?

About Lenormand Questions

The area of Lenormand questions raises some issues about how we as readers actually use the cards;, and what the implications of our choices are.

In this section, I look at getting yes/no answers from the cards, but also the question of fate and free will and how that impacts the kinds of questions we might ask. I also examine the sort of questions that get the best results, as well as how we can make sure the questions we are asking are as empowering as possible for us as individuals.

Positive & Negative Card Meanings: Answer Yes or No?

I should point out here that I'm not generally a huge fan of **Yes/No** Lenormanding, as personally, I find the approach a bit superficial and would rather get in-depth with the cards to get a complete answer to my questions.

However, there *are* times when, at the start of a reading, you might just quickly want an at-a-glance overall "Yes" or "No" feel of a spread.

How? Well, you can get one by looking at the predominance of positive or negative cards in answer to your particular question.

Positive Usually "Yes" cards – and reasons why they are
As well as the list below, I'm including the reasons *why* the following cards would usually be positive in response to a yes/no question.

Rider – Arrival

Clover – Luck, Good Fortune

Bouquet – Blessings, Gift

Stars – Hopes, Dreams, Wishes, Achievement

Dog – Friend, Support

Heart – Love, Warmth

Sun – Success, Happiness

Moon – Emotions, Creativity

Key – Answer

Fish – Abundance, Flow

Anchor – Stability, Certainty

Negative Usually "No" cards – and reasons why they are

Clouds – Uncertainty, negativity

Snake – Problems, negativity, betrayals

Coffin – Life drained, ending

Scythe – Cuts, pain. reduction

Whip – Challenges and conflicts

Fox – Something stolen

Mountain – Blocks, opposition, delays, No

Mice – Worries

Cross – Burdens and troubles

Which Cards Are NEITHER Positive or Negative?

Consider ALL other cards to be basically neutral. That's right – if they are not on the lists above, they do not generally have a particularly positive or negative connotation.

So, if you're doing a 3 card, 5-card, or 9-card reading:

- If you have **more positive cards than negativ**e the reading is tending towards the answer **Yes**. BUT be careful to read what the cards are actually saying too. See the **Other Factors** point below.
- If you have **more negative cards than positive**, then the reading is tending towards the answer **No**. But again, be sure to read the cards themselves to get the full message.

What If My Spread Has EQUAL Numbers of Positive/Negative Cards or Mainly Neutral Cards?

Generally speaking, this indicates that there really IS no overall yes or no answer, and there are other factors at play, such as your own efforts and input into the situation concerned. Use the information in the rest of the cards to make that call. And remember: There does come a time where you have to stop relying on cards to give you all the answers for your life. If you find yourself frustrated when it won't give you the answer or hope you want, or keep on asking and asking, it's a suggestion that it is YOU who needs to examine the situation, and wherever possible, start taking action yourself to drive what it is you want

Other Factors To Bear In Mind

The surrounding cards, positions and combinations of cards are also *extremely* important in any reading, regardless of the overall general positivity and negativity in the spread.

As you'll know from practicing your card combinations any negative-looking card can be tempered by a positive one and vice versa. Again, this is why I generally prefer *not* to do yes/no readings but rather to read the spread fully as it is. Card order and the actual cards involved can be incredibly important and make big differences to overall meanings. You could happily be assuming that something is a definite YES, for example, on seeing mainly lovely positive cards, when in fact there's actually big fat **Snake** card sitting at the end of your five card spread casting a dark squall over everything.

On the flip-side, you might find yourself filled with doom and gloom because you've got three or four negative cards, but then there's a lovely big **Sun** sitting at the end of your chain of cards, telling you to be positive, because it'll all most likely be OK in the end!

So it depends what your needs are, but personally, I would use the **yes/no** method rarely. It can be useful to get the overall feel for a question, but it isn't the whole story by any means.

Asking Lenormand Questions For The Best Results

Getting an accurate and useful reading with Lenormand is more often than not about making sure you get the question right. The overall message really is that you'll get out the quality that you put in.

You'll find that often if you ask a vague question (or don't ask one at all) you'll get a vague answer, or one that is just as vague when it comes to interpretation (And yes, the old adage is actually "ask a stupid question and you'll get a stupid answer" but I'm sure you get the picture!)

Why? Because the cards are often a reflection of what's going on inside your head and how clearly you can articulate the problem or issue at hand. "So within, as without," as they say. The **clearer** you are about what you're trying to find out, while at the same time being **open** to the true answers, the more likely it is that you will find what you seek.

The Basic Rules for Questions:

✤ Be specific
✤ Be direct
✤ Be clear
✤ Be prepared for and open to unexpected (or unwanted!) answers
✤ Try to use open questions rather than yes or no for more information
✤ Don't keep asking the same question just because you don't like the answer!
✤ Be ethical and think about why you're asking the question

What Are Open Questions And Why Are They More Useful In Readings?

Open questions are the opposite to 'yes/no' questions, where the answer will be either yes or no.

Yes/no questions can work but aren't always that helpful for Lenormand readings because they allow for less nuance and influence, and the useful bits of information that the storytelling nature of Lenormand can bring.

Sure, you can get a feel for whether the overall answer is likely to be 'yes' or 'no' from the spread of the cards but what is more *interesting* and informative about the reading in most cases is the **reasons** why or why not something is likely to go one way or another, the **factors** that are at play. It is these that form the deeper understanding of the issues that are at hand.

Open questions usually begin with one of the following:

How – ?
What – ?
Why – ?
Who – ?
Where – ?

For me, personally, I usually find the first three – **How, What and Why** (unless I'm specifically trying to find out the details or identity of a person) yield the best results.

Examples Of Good Questions To Ask

You should be as specific as you can with the details of your particular question, using names etc as appropriate, but here are some broad examples:

How is this visit likely to go? (not "Will the visit be awful?")
How can I best succeed in this endeavour? (not "Will I succeed in this endeavour?")
How can this problem resolve?
How did this issue arise?
What do I need to be aware of this week?
What blessings or positives are coming up for me this week?
What is going on with this person and me?
What is the key to this issue?
What do I need to consider if I – ?
Why is this person behaving the way they are?
Why did I not get that job?
Why have I not yet met my soulmate?
Why has this couple broken up?
Why has she not heard from this person?

LOZZY'S COMPLETE GUIDE TO LENORMAND

As you can see, it's helpful to use specific questions even if you are doing general readings

Questions and Ethics

This ties in with why you are asking what you're asking, and knowing and thinking about the sort of answers you might get and the issues you are dealing with. It's particularly important when you are reading for and about other people. When framing questions, I would always think about whether the answer's going to yield something helpful or respectful or ultimately empowering for them or others involved.

So "How can I make this person love me/What do I have to do to make this person love me?" for example, is neither empowering or ethical. The idea of "making" anyone do anything goes against the principle of free will, and the kind of desperation revealed in the question is likely to be at the root of what the real issue is. "How can I find love/ where am I likely to find love/Why haven't I yet met someone?/What are the issues between me and x?" is likely to uncover much more helpful and ultimately empowering information.

Likewise, I'd never ask direct questions about health or health outcomes (even though sometimes issues can pop up in readings); these are questions for qualified health practitioners, not card readers. Responsibility for someone's entire wellbeing or life path should ever be put in a reader's hands; ultimately the responsibility should always rest with the person themselves.

Not Asking The Same Question Over and Over

A lot of readers give almost mystical reasons for why you shouldn't keep asking the cards the same questions on the same topic again and again. As if the card are some sort of god or spiritual force who will punish you if you don't "follow the rules" or bow down to them sufficiently.

You may or may not have your own beliefs about the reasons why cartomancy works and the mechanisms and forces behind that, but for me I think the truth is much more grounded and simple. This is about **you** or the person you're reading for, and the answers and issues you – or they – are happy or not happy to accept as *possible*. Often in life, the things you are least happy to have to confront are the things you find that you most need to.

I have often found that reading the cards and getting an answer I didn't really like or wasn't hoping for forced me to consider possibilities, situations or pathways that I wouldn't have come across otherwise. And more often than not, the issues the cards turned up turned out in the long run to be absolutely correct, even if I didn't quite feel ready to face them at that time. It's almost as if the readings were simply reflecting what I knew subconsciously but didn't really want to yet acknowledge. The cards, I have found, are *very* good at giving warnings, although perhaps that's just me.

If you don't get the answer you want and keep asking over and over until you do, you diminish the effectiveness of this aspect of Lenormand as a tool. I do understand the instinct, but if you're just confirming what you already want to hear, you're not necessarily doing yourself any favours, or getting the most from the cards.

Ask it once, and be done with it. In the long run, you'll most likely be glad that you did!

Future, Fate & Free Will In Lenormand Readings

While not all Lenormand layouts *necessarily* have a 'telling the future' component, both the **9-Card** and the **Grand Tableau** in particular do. In the 9-card reading, the right-hand column is specifically said to reveal future influences. Similarly, in the Grand Tableau, anything to the left of the Querent card is said to relate to past or passing influences, and to the right of the Querent, upcoming influences.

That being the case, what are the different ways we as individuals might respond to the "future" parts of Lenormand readings – and how may we find it useful, if at all?

Should We Even Be Reading For the Future?

So what is the purpose of including possible future events or influences in our readings? Is it a good idea to even go down that route? After all, a lot more cartomancy professes to focus more on the personal development aspects than pure fortune-telling these days; prediction has become almost something of a dirty word. I do use it myself, but not in every reading, and even when I do, I have found some ways of responding to it and questioning it are more useful than others.

Personally, I think it's human nature to want to see into the future. I certainly don't think that it's all that systems like Lenormand have to offer, but fortune-telling has a long history for a reason, after all.

As human beings, we are pattern-seekers; our brains have evolved that way. We don't like to think of things being out of control, and we *really* don't like big gaps where we think answers should be. We are often especially uncomfortable with the idea that there isn't some kind of framework for the parts of life that are unknown to us. We want to know things like "Why are we here? Do we have a purpose as individuals? Do we have meaning? Are our lives important? Is there someone or something in charge of things here or is it all just random?" We try and create frameworks all the time to incorporate those things that seem unanswerable. Whether it's a traditional religion, or a more eclectic collection of spiritual beliefs – including ideas about Destiny and Fate.

How Useful Is The Idea of Fate in A Reading?

What is fate anyway? Is our destiny set in stone? Is it the case that whatever we do, our life is going to unfold exactly as has been ordained by some outside power ahead of time? Or are things a bit more complicated than that?

Your *beliefs* about fate can have quite an impact in a reading, both in the questions you ask and how you respond to a reading. You might believe, for example, that the future is already set in stone and you are just the passive recipient of it. You might ask questions like "Will I meet someone, or date this particular man?" "I want X to happen. Will it?" "Will I get this job? When?"

You might believe that there is no such thing as a set Fate, and everything that happens is a result of you exercising your free will. If you use cards at all, you'll tend to ask more 'depth' questions like, "What can you tell me about X situation in my life?" "What is useful for me to consider at the present time?"

Or you might, as I do, think that your destiny is largely in your own hands as above, a result of you exercising your own free will, and you have the power to influence it, but there are also certain life lessons on your path that you've already set in motion through your own past actions as well as those random, unexpected life events that get thrown at all of us.

At the same time, you exercise your free will in both having set them in motion in a way, and in responding to them AND to the possibility of them being told to you in the present. Doing a card reading is an act in itself, after all. The past and present are always connected to the future, and there are some strands that follow throughout your life (I often find, for example, the same 'themes' coming up again and again in my readings) but at the same time you are free to respond to their likelihood and their influences. "Ok, well what if this were to happen? Then what would I do?"

Will It/Won't It Questions

Although in the past, I have let myself be "tied" to what appears in readings sometimes, I haven't rarely found that a particularly helpful approach. Ironically, I find the "Will it/won't it?" destiny-set-in-stone type questions have been most useful to me only when the answer seemed to be a firm "No," remained resolutely open-ended, or urged me down a different path than the one I was hoping for!

After all, these questions are usually asked when the reader, deep down, really just wants the answer to be a "Yes." Often in a situation where there are barriers of some kind being thrown up.

Card readers will often get some variation of questions like, for instance, "Will I ever get together with X person?". But asking that question and making an effort to do or go as far as getting a reading already gives some clues as to the situation you're in. It generally implies a) you're not with X person now b) You really, really want to be with X person c) There is some barrier, like maybe you really like them but they haven't shown much interest, are with someone else, live far away, or whatever.

So what would be more useful to you in that case? A reading where it says "Yes!" (in which case what do you do in response? Sit at home and wait for them to fly in through the window and drop into your lap? Follow them around like a puppy? Cut off all your friends and sit by the phone waiting for them to call?). Or a reading that won't give a firm answer but suggests something along the lines of "Socialise more. Spend time with friends. Sign up for a college course" and so on?

My Own Experiences With "Fate"

This may just be me, but in my experience, the 'Fate' stuff that comes up as accurate most often tends to be those more random events parts of the reading that at the time you think, "Huh? That's out of place. Can't see how that's connected," and it isn't until later that you see that that's the very bit that turned out… a specific event, a person… to be spookily accurate all along. It's just that you didn't have the knowledge in your life at the time to be able to see it clearly (or perhaps didn't want to). I get this one a lot on Grand Tableaus. It's usually the kind of things outside of yourself that you don't have control over: those random events in life.

In terms of usefulness, though I find that it's better to see potential future influences as exactly that: *potential*, in the context of the overall reading including past and present, rather than something fixed. More like "If I carry on with this current way of thinking, these are the most likely influences coming up." Which then sets you on the path of thinking, "Okay, well, what might I do about that?" And then exercising your own free will.

What Does This Mean For Readings In Practice?

Well, first off, that generally speaking, it's usually not that useful to believe that everything is set in stone. It makes you too passive. It takes responsibility away from you and places it in the cards' or another reader's hands. At the end of the day, you are an active participant in your own life. Even if something comes up that you didn't want to hear, it should encourage you to take action, to open up other paths and consider other options. I never let readings dictate decisions to me. I choose and frame my questions carefully.

The most useful Lenormand readings, I find, give you information, but show where influences connect. In my own readings these days, I tend to go for the "depth" and "exploration" approach over pure fortune-telling and use that information to try to empower myself and others. Really, it's about guidance, not Fate.

What Do We Really Want?

Importantly, as a reader, it's worth questioning the question you're asking of the cards. What do you REALLY want to know and why? What answers are you looking and hoping for in your life? I like readings to open up possibilities, rather than close them down. To empower myself and others rather than to take away responsibility and hand it over to Fate. So it's always worth thinking about what **you** want to know, and what that's telling you about your life. For example:

✤ Are you scared of making a jump without a concrete answer? What actions can you take to make it less of a risk? Are there other factors you need to consider? Are there other ways you can get what you want without taking that risk?

✤ What would it mean if you weren't to end up married to that person? What would you do instead?

✤ What if you don't find fame and fortune down a particular road? Might there be other paths open to you instead? Or is fame and fortune actually not that important to you deep down?

✤ Do you want the cards to make a decision for you? Why? Why are you finding that particular decision difficult? Are there factors you are ignoring that you need to explore further in your day-to-day life? Are you just frustrated by a delay? What practical actions can you take to make that decision easier?

So always think about the questions you are asking and why.

Tips For Asking Empowering Lenormand Questions

So following on from that, let's talk a little more about specific ways you might ensure your experiences with Lenormand and other systems exercise as much of your free will as possible.

As many Lenormand layouts work best with specific questions in particular contexts, here's a tip list for making sure you are asking the Lenormand questions that are as empowering as possible, rather than leaving all things in your life to Fate.

1. Don't ask Yes/No questions

Essentially, the more "closed" answers are, the less power you have in them. Yes/no questions are mostly fatalistic, and usually, in the context of Lenormand and other cartomancy systems, start with the word "Will…?" Will this thing happen, yes or no?

Yes/No questions disempower you, because they assume that the future is fixed and there's nothing at all you can either do about it or to create new pathways into the future for yourself.

Instead of:
Will I meet someone in the next six months?

Try:
What can I do towards helping me meet someone new in the next few months?

2. Avoid "When?" questions

Asking for exact timing and timeframes is another way of keeping things closed and limited and not allowing for possibilities to unfold – including any pathways you might create yourself. Although I give you ways of using Lenormand timings in this book should you want to, I personally rarely give specific timings in my own readings, although do quite often limit their range to specific timeframes instead.

Again, asking "When will this happen?" questions implies that all events in life have already been predetermined by some outside force, along a very fixed timeline from which we cannot deviate. But the reality is that the future is most often created by actions we take in the present, along with the past influences and experiences we bring along with us, as well as the usual one or two random events that we couldn't possibly hope to control. There could be many possible future pathways, many possible future alternatives we can create. Sitting around waiting for things to drop into your lap, or worse, avoiding taking action because it doesn't fit into a designated, limited timeframe disempowers you and makes you a passive recipient in your own life.

Instead of:
When will I get a new job?

Try:
What are the steps I might take now towards getting a new job as soon as possible?

3. Ask more What/How/Why Questions

The most empowering Lenormand questions are usually exploratory and involve diving deep for information, having to think about things. The best way of doing that is to start your question with either What, How, or Why to gain more in-depth information.

Instead of:
Is this relationship worth pursuing? (a yes/no question)

Try:

What factors should I think about with regard to this relationship?

or

How might I improve how this relationship develops?

4. It's Your Life: Take Responsibility and Ownership for it

We all have things in life that we cannot control. Other people's desires, beliefs and actions. Random events. Late trains, car breakdowns, power cuts, bad weather, a crazy event on the news.

However, just as many things that happen in our lives as individuals are within our control. Weighing up big decisions with pros and cons, choosing to go with our gut feelings about something (or someone!), assessing whether or not something makes us feel good or bad and why and what we might do about it. Knowing and understanding ourselves and our reasons for doing things is a choice, knowing whether a situation is a good or bad one for us. Whether to try something 'just in case' or whether to not bother because 'there's probably no point anyway and I'll never succeed' is a choice you make that has direct impacts on what may or may not happen to you in future.

And sometimes life IS difficult. Nobody said it was going to be 100% easy at all times. Sometimes it's hard to know what to do or where we might take the next step. Sometimes you do have to sit down and work through things, and sometimes it isn't instantaneous. But if you hand over all the responsibility for your life to Fate (or the cards or, worse, attempt to make it that of a card reader, say, or astrologer) that really isn't a healthy level of empowerment

Instead of:

Handing responsibility for your life choices and your life events over to Fate, another person, a card reader/an astrologer to direct you and wait for things to 'just happen'

Try:

Using the cards in a more exploratory way. Gathering information about the world and influences around you, creating choices, thinking about possibilities, examining how the cards in a reading made you feel, taking action, believing the future is something you actively create. Take the reins!

5. Think About What's At The Root of Your Question & Why You Want To Know

When you ask a question of the cards, consider both why it is you are asking and what, deep down, you really want to know and what you want to achieve.

For example, an initial question about whether or not you should resign from your job is likely to have at its root a dissatisfaction with your current career and or life path. Are you feeling stuck in a rut? Why? What might you be able to do about it? Do you half feel like just handing in your notice tomorrow and telling your boss where to stick it, but that feels a bit dramatic? Are you deep down looking for ways to unstick yourself but that don't involve you doing something silly and making yourself homeless because you can't pay your rent?

The trick is to try and be as honest as possible with yourself about why you are asking what you are asking and why you have framed it in the way you have

Instead of:

Asking the cards whether you should do the big scary dramatic thing or not (yes/no) and handing over the power to Fate to make the decision for you

Try:

Using the cards to help YOU get to the root of the problem. The cards, I find, often reflect what is going on with me, not the uncontrollable world outside me (as within, so without). What factors and influences might you want to consider in helping find a solution to the problem?

6. Think What You Might Do With Various Answers

This relates to the previous point, and is another way of examining the root of the issue in front of you. I mean, what if you did ask a yes/no question and you got the answer you secretly wanted. Now what? What if the cards were to give you the opposite answer? What would you do then?

Instead of:

Waiting for the cards to give you all the answers

Try:

Thinking before you ask about "what if?" What actions would I take if my reading said this thing? What actions might I take if it said the opposite? "What if it tells me what I do want to hear? What if it tells me what I don't want to hear? What then?" How can you frame the question in a way that whatever answer the card gives, it empowers you and inspires you to action in some way?

7. Focus on Yourself & Your Life & Things YOU can do right now

The more you focus on other people (ie stuff you can't and shouldn't want to control) and the idea of a fixed, fated future (another thing you can't control) the less empowered you will be. Would you like somebody else trying to pull your strings? Nobody else but you is responsible for your life, and it's in your life that you can take the most action AND see the most results.

Instead of:

Using the cards to nose about others & things that aren't really your business & have little impact on your own life and things that are outside your control

Try:

Framing all your questions so they focus only on your own life and potential actions. "What might I need to consider about my relationship with X" is far more empowering (&way less sneaky) than "Tell me who X is thinking about right now?"

8. Make Questions Precise

As they say: ask a woolly question and you get a woolly answer!

Instead of:

What's coming up this week?

Try:

What areas of my life might I want to take action on this week?

9. Don't Ask the Cards to Make Big Decisions For You

Again, are you putting your future in the hands of the cards (or a card reader)? Are you handing them the power to make YOUR life decisions for you?

Instead of:

Putting your fate in the hands of the cards: "Should I do this or this? Just tell me what to do! I want to know – NOW!"

Try:

Using the information the cards give you about current influences to consider for yourself their impact on your life, your preferences and how you feel THEN weigh that information up along with all the other information around you before making decisions. Sometimes decisions aren't easy to make. Often, that's for very good reason, and that is normal and fine. And again, you should not be placing responsibility for your life decisions in the hands of other people because it seems easier just to hand it over. It isn't fair on them, and makes you a passive recipient in your own life.

10. Allow Yourself Time to Process What Has Come Up

Sometimes, the cards will tell you something unexpected or, more often, stuff you don't want to hear. "No, no," you might think, "That can't be right." Often because you don't want it to be. Let it brew for a bit.

Instead of:

Desperately reading and rereading the cards until you get the answers you want

Try:

Giving it a bit of time and considering what came up for you and why it has had an effect on you. Have you looked at the real root of what you were asking? Are there deeper themes or issues coming up in the situation that are worth exploring?

Telling A Story With Lenormand

The First Question To Ask Is—Should You? Do You Need To?

It is not always necessary to force the cards into a narrative, especially when you're doing readings for yourself . Sometimes, especially if you have left the context a bit open or general, and are just being broadly predictive, there's a chance that you might miss out on something vital if you try to impose too much of a narrative structure on it all. Almost as if you're trying to make it mean something it might not. Most of the time though, and particularly when you have a specific question or are reading for friends and family, it will help to give the cards extra meaning. Lenormand is a story-telling system, after all.

So How Can You Do It?

Well, given Lenormand is a language, there's a bit of an art to it, and yes, it involves some creative thinking and storytelling skills, and as we've said previously, the need to think intuitively about all the meanings too.

Remember, you are building the story of the cards from four main elements:

♣ The individual card meanings
♣ How they combine and their positions in the layout you have chosen
♣ The context of the reading
♣ The specific question you asked

EXAMPLE

Let's take a look at the same three cards in different situations, with different questions, and see how we might weave narratives out of each.

The General Question

Imagine you pull the following three cards for someone (deciding that it's going to be a card combination reading not a past-present-future) and the question is simply:

Q: What's Coming Up For Me This Week?

You pull the following three cards:

Snake—Ship—Ring

So we have our three cards and we know their basic meanings. We don't have a context, though, and it's just a very general question, so we're going to have to go with general meanings about travel and transport when we do this reading.

First, we look at the meanings individually:

Snake = a problem or betrayal of some sort
Ship = a journey or trip, movement, travel
Ring = agreement, committed relationship, deal or promise

If you just read these in a line as if they were words in sentence, you could get something like: *A problem on a journey involving an agreement, relationship or deal*

Now, we look at the cards in combination:

If we take the **Ship** as the keycard, and combine the mirrored Cards 1+3 around it, we get
Ship = A journey or trip at the centre of the reading, which is surrounded by **Snake-Ring** = Agreement or contract problem or betrayal. So:
An agreement or contract problem around a journey or trip.

Then, we can read Cards 1+2 and 2+3

Snake-Ship = journey or transport problems or betrayal

Ship-Ring = agreed or contracted journey

Travel problems on an agreed or contracted journey.

Worth thinking a bit about this one. Travel problems in general are easy to define and pretty common in day to day life but we don't have a context here at all. In particular, what kinds of journeys might be 'agreed or contracted'? Perhaps it is just a trip that has been pre-arranged or pre-booked? If that agreement is 'betrayed' might that indicate a cancelled trip?

Could be. That makes sense.

Okay, so:

Now we tie it all together in answer to our question:

Q: What's Coming Up For Me This Week?

A: A problem of some kind on an agreed or arranged journey. It's likely that travel plans and arrangements you've made will be disrupted in some way or an expected trip that's been arranged will be cancelled.

Do you see now why context and question can be so important? In the above example, we have no choice but to use the most general day to day and basic meanings for the cards that we can.

Now let's see what happens when we use the *same* three cards but with different questions and in different, more specific contexts.

The Money Question

Your friend Jenny is worried about her finances and wants to know if there's anything she needs to know in relation to that in the near future.

Q: What Does Jenny Need To Know About What's Coming Up With Her Finances?

Snake—Ship—Ring

The meanings individually:
This time, we know the context, so we can look at the cards in terms of that.

Snake = a problem or betrayal of some sort
Ship = something moving, transport or travel. In the money context, this can also mean a transfer.
Ring = agreement, committed relationship, deal or promise. As this means 'bond' it can also mean a payment.

So now we have our previous meaning but can give it a financial context.
A problem, possibly with a trip or with a transfer involving something agreed or a payment

The cards in combination:
Ship = A trip movement or transfer, which is surrounded by
Snake-Ring = Payment problem or betrayal
A payment problem around a transfer or a trip

Then, we can read Cards 1+2 and 2+ 3
Snake-Ship = journey or transfer problems or betrayal
Ship-Ring = agreed journey or payment transfer

Transfer problems on a payment OR a trip or transfer she can't get out of (direct debit? Standing order?) that causes problems

So there are a few possibilities here, really, with the Ship in the finance context. Either Jenny won't get a payment she's been expecting OR she'll have to pay for something she can't get out of and that will cause her problems.

Now we can answer our question:

Q: What Does Jenny Need To Know About What's Coming Up With Her Finances?
A: A problem of some kind on an agreed or arranged payment. Either Jenny won't get a payment she's been expecting or she'll have to pay for something she can't get out of and that will cause her problems.

Which one? I would leave that to Jenny and not impose it unless she gives you more information that clarifies the situation

The Career Question

Martin's been offered a job that involves a lot of travel. In deciding whether or not to take it, he wants to know more about the offer.

Q: What Should Martin Know About The New Job He's Been Offered?

Snake—Ship—Ring

The meanings individually:
So now we're in the career context with these meanings

Snake = A problem or betrayal of some sort, something not to be trusted.
Ship = Travel. Transfer, movement, move (So the travel aspect of the job is key.)
Ring = Agreement, contract, deal or promise (Job offer/contract)

So reading the cards in Martin's context, we get:
A problem with the travel involved in this offer or contract.

The cards in combination:
Ship = The work travel surrounded by
Snake-Ring = Agreement or contract problem or betrayal
A contract problem around the travel.

Then, we can read Cards 1+2 and 2+ 3
Snake-Ship = travel problems or betrayal
Ship-Ring = contracted, obligated or agreed travel

The travel aspect is clearly an issue, given as it contracted. Martin needs to think about what he'd be signing up to here. The Snake card indicates there is something amiss with both the travel and the agreement. The cards don't tell us what, but in the context it could be anything from unreasonable expectations of what is expected of him travel-wise, from a difficult commute, to who pays for travel .

Now we can answer our question:

Q: What Should Martin Know About The New Job He's Been Offered?
A: That there is a problem with the travel that is part of the contract. Martin needs to dig a little bit more into exactly what he'd be signing up to and check the small print before signing up to anything.

The Love Question

Sarah's been having trouble with her boyfriend since he's been away on a stag weekend. She wants to find out more.

Q: What's Going On With Sarah's Boyfriend?

Snake—Ship—Ring

The meanings individually:

So now we're in the love and person description context. Sarah is asking about a specific person so we need to think about the person-related meanings with this.

Snake = A problem or betrayal of some sort, someone not to be trusted. Other woman?

Ship = Travel. Traveller. Someone from overseas? Holiday? This'll be the stag weekend.

Ring = Promise, commitment, committed relationship, marriage, engagement.

So reading the cards in Sarah's context, we get.

A problem or betrayal with a trip, holiday or travel and a commitment.

The cards in combination:

Ship = Travel, trip, surrounded by

Snake-Ring = Agreement or commitment problem or betrayal

A betrayal or problem on the stag weekend.

Then, we can read Cards 1+2 and 2+ 3

Snake-Ship = trip betrayal

Ship-Ring = relationship trip - the stag weekend itself?

A commitment problem or betrayal that's arisen around this trip

Again, it depends on what you know about Sarah and her boyfriend so be careful about jumping to conclusions or being too definitive with any accusations. Either it's the most obvious explanation—he's cheated on her on the trip, OR the trip itself has done something to cause him to question their commitment. Maybe him going at all caused problems between them.

Now we can answer our question:

Q: What's Going On With Sarah's Boyfriend?
A: The trip has caused a problem with his commitment. He may have cheated on her, or the trip itself may have caused problems in their relationship. Sarah needs to do some digging: but the problem definitely has something to do with the stag weekend. She should focus on finding out more about what happened on the trip.

To sum up, then, the key to connecting the card meanings into a story is to build it using your knowledge of four main elements:
- ♣The individual card meanings
- ♣How they combine and their positions in the layout you have chosen
- ♣The context of the reading
- ♣The specific question you asked

Exercise VI
Telling Stories With Lenormand

This exercise is designed to help you practice telling stories in context with Lenormand. Here, we'll be using three cards to practice making a story from them for three different contexts and different meanings.

The Task:

- Look at the three cards given, and follow the steps to come up with a general interpretation.

- Write a few sentences pulling the information together in a way that makes sense in a general context, making sure to include the meanings of **each** of the cards and combinations.

- Now interpret the same cards in the specific contexts that follow, making sure to answer the questions given.

Question (General):

What Is Coming Up This Week?

Stork	**Whip**	**Bear**

Meaning: _____   _____   _____

Cards 1+ 3 Combined around Card 2

_____ + _____ around _____

Meaning: _____

Cards 1+ 2 Combined   _____ + _____

Meaning: _____

Cards 2+ 3 Combined   _____ + _____

Meaning: _____

Cards 1+2, 2+3 _____

Q: What Is coming Up This Week? (General)

A:

_____

_____

_____

Question (Career):

John wants a raise at work. What would you advise him?

	Stork	**Whip**	**Bear**
Meaning (Career)	_____	_____	_____

Cards 1+ 3 Combined around Card 2

_____ + _____ around _____

Meaning: _____

Cards 1+ 2 Combined _____ + _____

Meaning: _____

Cards 2+ 3 Combined   _____ + _____

Meaning: _____

Cards 1+2, 2+3   _____

Q: John wants a raise at work. What would you advise him?

A:

_____

_____

_____

Question (Relationships):

Your daughter's upset about her relationship. What's been going on?

Stork	**Whip**	**Bear**

Meaning (Relationship) _____   _____   _____

Cards 1+ 3 Combined around Card 2

_____ + _____ around _____

Meaning: _____

Cards 1+ 2 Combined   _____ + _____

Meaning: _____

Cards 2+ 3 Combined   _____ + _____

Meaning: _____

Cards 1+2, 2+3   _____

Q: Your daughter's upset about her relationship. What's been going on?

A:

_____

_____

_____

You can check your answers **on p. 294.**

So What About Lenormand Timings?

A lot of my readers ask about Lenormand timings, so I wanted to give guidance in this book although, as mentioned earlier, generally speaking, I don't personally tend to use timings much, mainly because I don't believe our futures are completely fixed, and don't like to limit possibilities that severely. If I'm interested in restricting my reading to a particular time period, I tend to put it into the question e.g. "What are the biggest influences coming up in the next three months?" kind of thing instead.

Nonetheless, I know many feel differently, so I will give you the information and leave it up to you as to whether you choose to use it or not. I will also give you some ways that you might like to experiment with in practice.

It's also worth pointing out that there's more than one 'official' method of reading the card timings, and it is not as simple as it may at first appear, so please bear this in mind, experiment, and if you choose to do so, see what works for you.

So first off, which cards are we talking about? Do all of the cards have a possible timing meaning or not?

Let's find out.

Lenormand Card Timing Meanings

There are three main ways you can use the cards for timing in terms of individual card meanings:

✤ The card number (1-36)
✤ The card symbol itself if it indicates, say, a particular time or season

❖ Any 'event' symbolised by the card. This can be a place, a feeling, an event

You are unlikely to find the last on many 'lists' but in my view, one of the best and most useful ways to indicate timings, rather than exact dates and times, is in the context of 'events' told by the cards combined. I'll be covering this in more detail in the next section.

So some example timing meanings:

Rider One. Soon, Next, One Day, Week, Month, First of the Month, January, On a Visit
Clover Two. February, Two Weeks, Days, Months, Second of the Month, By Chance
Ship Three. March, Three Weeks, Days, Months, Third of the Month, On a Trip or While On the Move
House Four. April, Four Days, Weeks, Months, When At Home
Tree Five. May. Five Days, Weeks, Months. Fifth of the Month, When All Is Green
Clouds Six. June, Six months, Weeks, Days, Sixth of the Month, When it's raining or overcast
Snake Seven. July, Seven Days, Weeks, Months. Seventh of the Month, During a Negative Event
Coffin: Eight. August, Eight Days, Weeks Months, Eighth of the Month, After An Ending
Bouquet: Nine. September, Nine Days, Weeks, Months. Ninth of the Month. Spring
Scythe Ten. October, Ten Days, Months, Weeks, Tenth of the Month Harvest time, Suddenly
Whip Eleven. November, Eleven Days, Weeks, Months, Eleventh of the Month, During Hard Times
Birds Twelve. December, Twelve Days, Months, a Year, Annual, Twelfth, Through A Conversation

Child Thirteen Days, Weeks, Months. Thirteenth of the Month, When New To Something, In Childhood

Fox: Fourteen Days, Weeks, Months, Fourteenth of the Month, At Work

Bear: Fifteen Days, Weeks, Months. Fifteenth of the Month, When Safe

Stars: Sixteen Days, Sixteenth of the Month, A Clear Night, At Night

Storks: Seventeen Days, Weeks, Seventeenth of the Month, Change of Season, During Change

Dog: Eighteen Days, Eighteenth Day of the Month, With Friends

Tower: Nineteen Days, Weeks, Nineteenth of the Month, In a Building or Official Place

Garden: Twenty Days, Weeks, Twentieth of the month, Outdoors

Mountain Twenty-One. Three Weeks, Twenty-One days, Twenty-First. Winter, When Alone

Crossroads: Twenty-two days, weeks, twenty-second of the month, When a choice is presented

Mice Twenty-Three Days, Twenty-Third, Very Soon, Rapidly, When Feeling Anxious

Heart Twenty-Four Days, Twenty-Fourth, Summer, During a Romance or when in love

Ring Twenty-Five. Continual, Repeated, Twenty-Five days, Twenty-Fifth , Once Committed or Agreed

Book Twenty-Six. Unknown, Hidden; Twenty Six Days, Twenty-Sixth, When You Know

Letter Twenty-Seven Days, Twenty-Seventh of the Month, When There's Notification

Man Twenty-Eight Days or the Twenty-Eighth of the Month

Woman Twenty-Nine days or the Twenty-Ninth of the month

Lily Thirty days, Thirtieth of the month. A long time. Winter. Later in Life

Sun Thirty-One days, A Month, 31st, Daytime. Dawn. A hot summer

Moon Lunar Cycle, Tidal, Evening, At Night. In your dreams.

Key Now. Eternal. All Time.

Fish In February/March (Pisces time). When independent.

Anchor Lifelong, a Lifetime. Forever. When stable.

Cross Long-Lasting, Ongoing. When burdened.

How might you actually use timings in a reading?

Like a lot of Lenormand, how you use the cards with regard to timing is fairly flexible; there are no set rules, but there's a range of ways you can do it to best effect.. Some options include pulling a single card or cards to answer the specific "When will...?" question, to using the playing card pips (again!) attached to a reading you're already doing, giving the likely series of events in a series of cards more like in a story.

Let's look in a little more detail. Here, I'll look at the numerous ways you can read Lenormand cards for timings—as well as some of the problems with "timing" readings, not least some of the assumptions that can be made that can limit the usefulness of your readings.

So take a look at some of the different methods here:

1. Put Timing Into The Question By Asking About What Will Happen In A Time Period

For this, you don't need to use any of the card timing meanings at all; the idea of a time period is included already in the question. So, for instance:

- ❖ What's coming up for me in the next 6 months?
- ❖ What's the biggest thing that is likely to happen to me this week?
- ❖ Name one positive thing that will happen to me today?
- ❖ What am I likely to see coming up in my love life in the next three months?
- ❖ What does the next year hold for me?

2. Use A Reading Type That Already Tends To Cover A Time Period

Some reading layouts tend to have an element of future time already embedded, and also tend to cover certain time periods.

❖ **9 Card Spread.** The right-hand column generally represents "near future" influences. It depends on the question, but generally, I find it covers the next few weeks and sometimes a month or two, but nearly always within two to three months.

❖ **The Grand Tableau.** The Grand Tableau overall nearly always covers periods of between six months to a year. Don't ask me why, it just does, although it should be noted that you don't HAVE to have it time-based at all. It can, like the 9-Card spread, cover past, present and future (with the position of the Querent card denoting the "present" column, any cards to the left, the past and any to the right, the future). Or you can specify that you want it to solely cover future influences. The cards in the left hand columns would then cover nearer future and moving further on in time as you read rightwards along the columns. For a year, then, this would mean each column of a 9 x 4 Grand Tableau reading represents a time period of approximately six weeks

3. Add Timing Into Any Reading Of A Question About Something Else

Generally, this is for "Will I… and when?" type questions, which are by far the most common types of question people ask when they're looking for future predictions.

Now, obviously, this kind of question includes many assumptions – particularly the idea that our futures are fixed and predestined along a very rigid timeline and we have no influence on them whatsoever. As I've said, I don't personally believe this, I'm afraid. I think it's limiting.

Also, you'll find that "When will I… and when?" type questions nearly always involve a desire and an assumption that the answer is going to be "Yes." But the real answer may not necessarily be yes at all. It may be "no" or "maybe" and therefore you may well not get the most accurate or useful reading if you try to read timings this way

The other problem here is that a standard reading is likely to have many cards included, with many potential times indicated on top of what the cards are actually saying in terms of their meanings in relation to the question. How on earth would you sort through them all to come up with some kind of timing?

You will likely find that trying to use the 'timing' meanings in a layout when you have lots of cards is not necessarily particularly helpful. It's the cards themselves that really tell more of a story and open up possibilities for a future – and a future that may or may not be fixed at that.

4. Do a Reading Specifically For the Timing Question

A far better method on timing is to carry out a reading *just* for the timing. To avoid the kind of confusions I mention above, I would also keep it short: just one card, say, or up to a maximum of three cards. Here are some examples:

Q: When Will I See My Friend Again?

Card pulled: 1. Rider
Answer: *Very Soon, in a day or so*

Card pulled: 31. Sun
Answer: *In The Summer OR on the 31st*

OK, so imagine I do this. What about more cards? Now, let's imagine I had had some money promised to me. So I know this money is coming and some time soon, but I am not sure when it is going to arrive. I ask the cards and pull three to answer this specific question.

Q: When Will My Money Arrive?
17. Storks—31. Sun—30. Lily

How might I answer this question with these cards?

I Could Use The Timing Meanings

I have quite a lot of options here and am going to have to use my intuition to suit both the cards and the situation. The three cards have all of the following options:

* Card 1: Seventeen Days, Weeks, Seventeenth of the Month, Change of Season, During Change
* Card 2: Thirty-One days, A Month, 31st, Daytime. Dawn. A hot summer
* Card 3: Thirty days, Thirtieth of the month. A long time. Winter. Later in Life

Now, looking at the cards, it it immediately strikes me that, timing-wise, we've got two seasons there, and a card that represents a change of season. None of the cards appears to represent a specific month, although two of them represent approximately a month in timespan. The most obvious interpretation for me would be *When The Season Changes From Summer To Winter.* It could also, perhaps, be *17 days and two months*.

But you'll see that even with a list of timing meanings in front of you, it's not obvious. You really do need to use your intuition to read the cards and make sense of them.

I Could Read The Same Cards As A Series of Events

The other thing you can do in answer to timing questions is treat the cards as a *series of events* that need to happen. So rather than assigning specific timeframes, dates or timing meanings, instead, you can look at the cards in terms of likely events or happenings

Q: When will my money arrive?

17. Storks—31. Sun—30. Lily

A: After a change (Storks) in the summer/or to a positive mindset (Sun) to do with age, experience or someone older (Lily)

Let's try this method with different questions and cards.

Q: When will I meet this person again?

7. Snake—17. Storks—24. Heart

A: When negativity or betrayal (Snake) has changed (Storks) into love (Heart)

Q: When am I likely to get a job?

22. Crossroads—1. Rider—33. Key

A: When the choice or options ahead (Crossroads) deliver or present (Rider) the answer (Key)

So personally, I find the last option the most effective and useful method by far, but you may find differently. The only way you're going to really know, though, is to try it out for yourself, keep a record, and see what happens!

Common Mistakes When Reading Lenormand Cards For Yourself

I read cards for myself regularly - and find them a useful personal tool. That said, some readers avoid this and only read for friends and family, taking the view that they're just too close to situations to be able to get a truly objective view.

Personally, I think reading for yourself regularly is a fantastic opportunity to develop a more intuitive and confident relationship with your cards, to experiment, see how they operate and to get them to work for you.

There are some pitfalls though that you're likely to come across in the course of your daily practice. Here are some of the main mistakes to avoid when reading for yourself, especially when you are starting out.

Not Being Objective

I talk a lot about developing your intuition, getting to know your cards and their meanings and how they work for you given what you know about circumstances, and trying not to second guess yourself. At the same time, you need to avoid being so subjective that you start changing those underlying meanings of the cards entirely. This is particularly true when you are asking a specific question and can, I know, be extremely tempting when the cards throw up an answer you don't really want to hear. Getting this right can be a delicate balancing act.

Ways To Be More Objective

I stand firmly by my advice to understand how each cards' meaning tends to manifest in your life. That said, at the end of the day, the cards that appear in your particular reading and for the question you have asked, are the cards that are there, and I like to think that they've appeared for a reason. Often, you'll find they throw up big surprises that can amaze you when you look back. My tip would be to go through your readings systematically, making sure you give equal weight to each card according to the layout you are using, and then try to imagine you are reading for somebody else. With practice and time, you'll start to see the patterns in how they manifest, which'll put you in a position where you can get the cards working for you.

Reading When Over-Emotional

This goes hand in hand with the advice above about staying objective. Extreme emotion is the opposite of objectivity and if you're reading cards when you're feeling highly emotional or in desperate or very upsetting situations where the stakes are very high, you are likely to cloud your interpretations with all your wishes and fears about the situation. Often, this is because these are situations that, by their very nature, are ones where you may not like the answers you are given. Lenormand can help with guidance, and often throws up underlying issues that are helpful to know and explore, but you have to be ready for that and to receive them. Situations of high emotion are often that way because there are things to work through and that are difficult to face. Lenormand-reading requires a cool, calm head. Wait until you are in a position where you can step back a bit from things.

Not Asking Clear & Precise Questions

It depends what you want from the cards, of course, if you are just doing very general predictive readings for yourself for practice, or if you have something very specific you want to know, but as we have seen, context and question really does affect how the card meanings manifest and how accurate they are. Over time, and with practice, you will start to see how the meanings have manifested in different situations.

Reading Again Because You Don't Get The Answer You Wanted

This relates to the need for objectivity and a clear head. The cards will show what they show. You may like it, you may not, but it's still giving you useful information. If you read the cards again, over and over, until you get the result you want, you've diluted what they're telling you. If you already know the only answers you'll accept, there seems little point in reading the cards at all. If this is you, you want to think about why it is you have the urge to do this. People often use tools like cartomancy in the hopes of confirmation of their wishes and needs; in a way, as a kind of control. If you find you're wanting to do this, the experience is still telling you something loud and clear: it's telling you what it is you want so much and that you're so rigid about that you're not ready to accept any alternative!

That said, the emotion you experience in this kind of situation is very useful information to have at your fingertips. Is this rigidity about the issue something you need to explore further, perhaps outside of cartomancy systems like Lenormand?

Treating Lenormand As Fixed Rather Than a Tool

Following on from that is the more philosophical question of why we're using Lenormand and other cartomancy systems in the first place, and whether we're clinging to interpretations and predictions in unhealthy ways. It's always a balancing act when it comes to predictive systems and the issue, in particular, of free will. Personally, I think our lives do follow overall patterns and are interconnected, and some things will happen whatever, but I'm also a huge believer in having control over our own destiny; I believe we largely create our own destinies through the choices we make in response to possibilities and events that happen in life.

How I Use Lenormand

I tend to use Lenormand in this way and the universal card meanings as a kind of framework, but I don't cling to it, and do my best to use the information my readings impart as a tool rather than let a given interpretation dictate my life and actions. That said, I have often found when I read for myself that the cards tell me stuff that deep down, I already know. For me, it's more that it's opened the possibility of making sure I truly consider the answers given. The cards have also been great for giving me warnings that I've found highly pertinent at times. Quite often they've led me to consider alternative possibilities that have ended up opening new pathways in my life.

I've also had numerous experiences where a reading did tell me something so precise either ahead of time or about something I really didn't know in a way that was uncanny. A practice reading about a usually highly confident friend that showed upcoming depression and illness (and no, I didn't share it, and yes, to my surprise it absolutely came to pass a year or so later. All I could do is be there when it did.). A reading about a man I knew that showed an investigation by an official body that I had no idea about (my response "Huh? He's being investigated?" was answered months later by the same person being fired from their job as a result of said and now revealed undercover investigation.) In any case, I think it's really important to try to find balance between the two.

The Benefits of Practice and Keeping A Journal!

Again, I truly believe that the best way to get the most out of Lenormand is to experiment with your readings, to find both what works and yes, which also means giving yourself the freedom to be wrong from time to time! Keeping your own

Lenormand journal and building it up with your own readings and personal insights is a great way to do this and find the best ways of using the system as a tool that eventually works for you.

My top tips for reading Lenormand for yourself:

❖ Be objective and clear-headed
❖ Avoid reading Lenormand when highly emotional
❖ Ask precise questions
❖ Accept and be open to the answers given
❖ Practice, and treat your personal readings as a tool.

Keeping A Lenormand Journal

So what do you need in order to start a journal? What *is* a Lenormand journal? A handwritten or even electronic notebook specifically for the purpose, in which you can jot down your personal notes and experiences with the cards, the card meanings, and record your regular readings - as well as the results! You might even wish to include sketches or photographs of the symbols or your own ideas for your own version of the cards.

Exercises To Try For Your Lenormand Journal

Getting To Know The Cards

Getting to know the cards and their meanings individually and becoming confident in your interpretations of them is key to your success with whole Lenormand system. So it's a good idea to spend some time looking at each and every card and really considering its underlying meaning. Obviously this is something you'll need to do over a period of time, and won't be something you complete overnight, but I would personally dedicate a section of your journal just to card meanings. My suggested exercise follows what I discussed earlier about getting confident with card meanings.

❖ For each card, have a page for it, and make notes about the following: The features of that symbol - person, thing or animal - in real day to day life

❖ The underlying meaning or sense that connects all of those things, in one or two words or phrases

❖ Ways that underlying meaning might manifest in, say, a) your own personal daily life b) in an individual's personality c) in a business or work situation d) in a relationship, or any other situation or context you're interested in.

Daily 3-Card Spreads

Not counting individual cards, the three-card spread is the simplest Lenormand reading you can do and is great for starting to practice basic card combinations, as well as getting a feel for how the card meanings manifested in your own daily life. I'd suggest doing at least a week of daily 3-card spreads,

Every day for a week:

❖ First thing in the morning, ask the cards "What is the main thing that will happen to me today?" draw three cards, and record them in your journal.

❖ Jot down a very basic interpretation of the cards, based on the linked card method (the 2nd) in my step by step guide to the Three-Card Spread

❖ In the evening, revisit the cards, and jot down the main events of the day. How relevant was your morning's interpretation of the cards to events?

Weekly 5-Card Spreads

I personally tend to read the cards weekly for the week upcoming as a part of my own Lenormand practice. Once you've got comfortable with the three-card spreads, you can move on to the 5-Card Layout, which is my personal favourite. Why? Because it is both simple and gives a fair amount of detail, while being straight to the point and not overwhelming. It's a bit much for a daily reading, but ideal for getting a picture of the coming week.

At the start of every week:

- ♣ Either on a Sunday night or Monday morning, ask the cards "What are the main things coming up for me in the next week?".
- ♣ Shuffle and draw the five cards and record them in your journal.
- ♣ Write down your interpretation of the cards, following the step by step guide to the 5-Card Layout
- ♣ At the end of the week, revisit the cards and your interpretation and note the relevance to the events of your week.

Biographical Readings

This is a fun way of practising the 9-Card Spread, and also the cards as they relate to people. For this exercise, I would pick either a celebrity OR, for even more of a challenge, a famous historical figure. Make it someone who you don't know all that much about, but who you could quite easily research online.

Biographical reading:

- ♣ Pick your celebrity or historical figure. Find an image of them, and just focus on the image for a bit. DON'T do any research at this point, but make sure you are focused on them and they are at the forefront of your mind.

❖ Now take your Lenormand deck and shuffle the cards, keeping that person in mind. Ask the cards to tell you about this person. You will be using either the Woman or the Man card as the focus card in this reading, and you will be putting it at the centre of a 9-card spread.When you feel ready, pull out your nine cards and lay them out in the 3x3 format with your Woman or Man card in the centre. I usually locate my keycard in the pack and then pull out the cards either side of that to build the layout. Use whatever method you feel comfortable with.

❖ Follow the step by step guide to the 9 card spread to build up the full picture. NB if it is a dead historical figure, they obviously don't have a future as such. In that case, rather than past-present-future, I would take the first column as their background, the middle as the point in time they're most famous for, and the future for what happened to them in the end.

❖ After you have completed your reading, do a little biographical research, using Wikipedia, for instance. How accurate was your reading in giving you information about this person?

The Next 6 Months

This is an advanced reading only, and I'd strongly suggest waiting until you've had plenty of practice particularly with reading card combinations, and both the 5-Card and 9-Card layouts, as otherwise, you might find it a little too overwhelming. Just as you did for the Daily 3-Card and Weekly 5-Card, you're going to be using a Lenormand layout for predictive purposes in your own life and recording it and the eventual outcome. The ideal layout for a reading of this sort is the Grand Tableau. I've picked the next six months as I've personally found the Grand Tableau to be a bit much even for a month. There is so much detail to be had here, and it's so involved that you need a decent stretch of time to really get the benefit of the effort you'll put in doing the reading. Also, the shorter the timeframe, the more diluted the meanings tend to be: it seems like way too much hard work to put in for what are only going to be relatively muted meanings and just a few weeks.

At the beginning of a six month period:

January and the start of June are obviously ideal times to do this exercise. Make sure you give yourself plenty of time to do this reading - it can easily take a whole day.

- ♣ Ask the cards "What is coming up for me in the next six months?"
- ♣ Shuffle and then when you're ready lay out all 36 cards in either the 9 x 4 or 8x 4 +4 layout of the Grand Tableau
- ♣ Following the step by step instructions in How To Read The Grand Tableau read the layout, making careful notes as you do so.
- ♣ For the in-depth part of the reading, I would focus solely on the main aspects of your life that you're interested in, which will be personal to you
- ♣ During the six months, do make a note in your journal of whenever anything happens that is relevant to the reading. At the end of the six months, have a check-in session with yourself and review your reading. How did it manifest in reality, and what does this tell you about your relationship with the cards?

Building Up To Reading For Other People

While the majority of those starting to read Lenormand are happy to just read for themselves, the time comes, of course, where quite a few of you would like to start reading for others. Or perhaps you have other people asking you to "do them a reading." What's the best way to get yourself to the point where you'd be comfortable to do so?

Learning Lenormand is a process, a gradual building-up. Nearly all would-be readers come to Lenormand from Tarot, so most of you will have some familiarity with the concept of card-reading itself, but it's worth underlining again: **Lenormand is a**

completely different system from Tarot, so in many ways, you will need to start from scratch.

What would be the main stages to take yourself through in order to build up to being able to read for others?

Get Familiar With The Cards' Meanings & Main Layouts & Read Regularly For Yourself

As above, the very first thing you'll need to do is build your confidence and familiarity with the cards' meanings, combinations and how the cards together work in readings. And the single best way to do that is practising regular readings for yourself.

Do the simple readings suggested above, like daily **3-card reading**s or simple 3-Card readings about situations in your own life.

Then when you're ready, move to **5-Card spreads** for more detail. Try readings with different kinds of questions. Apply the cards to different contexts in your own life. Try **9-Card spreads** to seek out information. And make sure you do a few **Grand Tableau**s for yourself.

Reflect On Your Accuracy, And Reading Strengths & Weaknesses

Learning Lenormand is not just about passively taking in information from card readers though; you need to be active about your own learning in order to build your own relationship with the system.

Do take the time to look back on your own readings over a period of time and reflect on them. The helpful thing about doing a bunch of readings about yourself is that nobody knows you and the realities of what goes on in your life better than yourself. And if it turns out you have got things wrong in your readings, no harm done: it's simply something to learn from and very useful information.

Here are some of the things you might reflect on:

❖ How accurate or useful did your interpretations turn out to be? Was there anything you missed that you can now see staring you in the face?

❖ On the other hand, were there things that you got totally wrong or you still don't know what the cards were referring to? What might you learn from that?

❖ We often find that meanings tend to work in certain ways for us in particular situations. How did the meanings tend to work for you and in which circumstances? Which layouts & methods worked best for you?

❖ Which cards give you trouble or seem to speak to you most? What was the most helpful way you found to use them day-to-day?

❖ Once you've done that, you can start plugging the gaps, perhaps reading further, or exploration on the issues that cause you difficulties.

Do Practice Readings Where You Can Check the Answers

This is something I used to love doing when I was learning, and sometimes still do to keep myself on my toes; looking at other people's readings and spreads, trying them out for myself, and THEN finding out what the 'answer' was. Either in reality or their interpretations.

As I've said, the great thing about reading for yourself is that you know yourself and your life and you can see quite easily where your readings went well, and where they fell short. But the less great thing about reading for yourself is that it's hard to be objective and keep emotional distance.

One of the BIGGEST skills to learn before you can start reading well for others is to be able to step back with a cool head and no personal investment at all and just read the damn cards as they are. To be totally objective. And then to see if you captured everything that needed to be captured in the reading. Lots of people put up their readings online, so it's always worth taking a look for yourself

And this is the number one reason I like to include *lots* of practice readings in my books - with answers & interpretations. If this is where you're at, you should find the practice readings at the end of this book helpful.

Do Readings *About* Others You Know

Once you've got practiced in that more distanced way of reading, it's time to get back to your own life again; but this time try doing readings ***about* the people around you**.

It's kind of half and half: there are probably things you know about them and their situations which you can bring to the readings, but this time, it's not about you. Something you're curious about? Got a question on a situation a friend is having? Do a reading, keep it to yourself—but then see what unfolds around you.

As with your own readings, see what worked and what didn't. What came up? What does that tell you for next time? What might you do differently? Try it.

And now is the time to start considering the other aspects too. Reading for others is a big responsibility. What sort of things would you have to be careful about when reading for another person? Imagine they were sitting in front of you. What sort of sensitivities might you need to have or think about in how you gave the reading? What would you do and not do? What questions wouldn't you answer? What sort of layouts would you use and why?

Let Go of Lists & Start Letting Intuition Guide You

Once you've got to this stage, you should be building much more confidence. Yes, you may still refer to lists like the Card Combinations from time to time, but if you've been thorough in your practice, you should be building up a strong relationship with your cards.

Now is the time to see if you're able to do without the lists and rely more heavily on your own knowledge and intuition. If you have someone sitting in front of you, you're not going to be spending all your time looking up combinations in a book or on a website. So now, see if, in your own readings or those about others, you can focus on the story the cards seem to be telling you, and how *you* might tell it.

Start Doing Practice Readings For Willing Friends & Family

It's up to you how you'd start to do this and at which stage. Many people don't read for others at all, so that is a decision you'd need to make for yourself based on what you've learned about your readings and your preferences so far. It's not for everyone, and it's way more about the interaction and the other person than it is about you, and involves a lot of skills, so it can be quite a leap.

One thing I would say if you do, is to **pick your people** carefully at this stage. It's best to keep things light-hearted; probably a friend or family member who's willing to help you out and do it out of curiosity and "for entertainment purposes", not someone in the middle of a massive breakdown. Avoid very emotionally loaded situations, and avoid being 'handed' responsibility for something that someone either needs to deal with themselves, or needs to see someone about (I'm thinking particularly about health issues or legal questions here.)

Also you need to consider practicalities. Are you going to be talking in person (in which case, be very confident) or dropping them an email? (I often do "distance" readings for people, which gives me more time to consider). How are you or the person going to choose the cards? Are they going to be shuffling them or are you? What deck will you be using? Which layout? How are you going to find out their question and frame it in a way that gives your reading focus? How are you going to keep yourself objective?

Ultimately, building up to reading for others is about building up your own confidence and own personal practice with the Lenormand cards, combining what you learn on here and other places with your own quirks and your own personal take on life.

So in brief then. Building up to reading for other people involves:

- ✤ Reflecting on your own experiences. Your accuracy, strengths and weaknesses.
- ✤ Getting familiar with card meanings & layouts, and reading regularly for yourself
- ✤ Doing practice readings where you can be totally objective and check the answers.
- ✤ Doing readings *about* others you know, and starting to think about how you would frame them.
- ✤ Moving from lists and books to using your own intuition
- ✤ Beginning doing "for entertainment purposes" readings for willing family and friends

A Note About Choosing Lenormand Decks

Finally, and since I'm hoping you aim to develop a strong relationship with your cards, I wanted to write about how to go about choosing which deck to use. There are loads of Lenormand decks currently on the market, and new ones being created all the time. This includes the standard or most popular decks, which are widely available as well as a range of decks created by artists which can be highly individual and often very beautiful, although often a bit more pricey. You could also make your own, of course, either by drawing them yourself, using photographs, or even, at the most simple, just the relevant playing cards with a print of the words on them.

Different readers may want different things from their cards. I've obviously got my own opinions and preferences with regard to decks—the one I started off with is the **Lo Scarabeo** deck— but I wanted to take a look at the questions that all readers should be asking in order to choose the best Lenormand deck for themselves.

Are The Central Images Clear?

This is the number one consideration for me, and the key, really, to what the Lenormand system is and isn't. Lenormand is not like the Tarot, and the deck you choose to use should never change the meaning of the core underlying symbols in any way. The fundamental meaning of each Lenormand card should be the same from deck to deck. Thus, a Clover card means "Luck" regardless of whether it be a simple drawing of a 4 leaf clover, a computer-generated graphic, a beautifully designed piece of artwork including a whole field of clovers, the flower or the leaves, someone holding a clover, or even just a plain print of the word itself.

Bear in mind that NO additional images that may appear in the card will ever have any bearing on that underlying meaning, and they would be completely irrelevant to it. Thus, a picture of a Snake wrapped around a tree is still the Snake card. The tree has no relevance and should not be included in the interpretation. A picture of a House at the end of a long winding path and with a lush garden is just a House; the rest has no relevance for that particular card.

This being the case, whatever you choose, it's important that it's very quickly clear to you as reader exactly what that card represents. Personally, I prefer uncluttered cards which only show the core image, large and centred, and that don't distract me with additional imagery. I would strongly suggest the same for beginners to avoid any confusion. There are certain cards in the deck that some readers look for the nuance in (for example, the directions that the symbol is facing, light and dark sides on a picture of a cloud) and if that is you, then you might like to consider those when choosing the images.

Do You Want A Traditional or Modern Design?

This is one consideration that really is down to personal preference, I think, and often down to your relationship with the cards, and how superstitious you tend to be around authenticity.

Many readers feel that a traditional-style deck with 18th century imagery and insets is more authentic and "proper" and helps brings them closer to the tradition of the cards themselves and their beginnings; other readers don't factor that in at all, finding that it's the core underlying meanings that connect them to the cards. Again, this would be down to whatever works best for you, how you best connect with the cards and what best prompts your intuition. Neither traditional or modern is inherently better, in my view, except that some modern decks can be too cluttered and attempt to add meanings and nuance that aren't really what the cards are about. So I am halfway between a modernist and a traditionalist on this, really.

One thing I would say is that given I see the Lenormand as a system of core and universal underlying meanings , I personally think the Lenormand system stands pretty well as is and does not generally require new interpretations or "nuanced" additions. I tend in particular not to go for "new guru" versions which are really adaptations of the fundamental system, or even sometimes an attempt at creating a whole new system which is seen as "better." So just as I would always go only for simplicity in the core symbols, I would also always only stick with the fundamentals. But that's just me.

Is The Beauty Or Design Of The Artwork Important To You?

Similar to the question about traditional or modern designs, if you are of an artistic or creative bent, you may find that a particular style or design draws you "into" the cards a lot more, and makes connecting with their meanings easier. You will see that there is a whole range of possible styles and designs. I prefer things to be bold yet simple, although I also love colourful cards. I also happen to be a fan of art deco and early 20th century design, so I do tend to go for that kind of look in the decks I choose.

But again, these kind of preferences are up to you. I would always choose something that "feels like me," if you see what I mean, but always with the need for those core card meanings at the forefront.

How Many Cards Are There In The Deck?

A traditional Lenormand deck has 36 cards, including one Man and one Woman card.

Decks which have more than 36 cards tend to be:

❖ Those which add extra people cards or which have alternate versions of standard cards, as the more traditional decks tend to be very Eurocentric.
❖ Expanded versions of the traditional deck with additionally-created nuanced meanings.

Personally, I'm happy with only the 36 card meanings in a standard deck, although I can understand the need for additional people cards occasionally, and certainly in situations where the supposed "Querent" cards aren't all that relatable to the reader. Again, though, this is personal preference. Bear in mind that for all decks with additional cards other than people, it is ONLY those decks that those cards appear in and you won't find them elsewhere. In most decks, these are optional. I'd suggest using these additional optional cards only if you genuinely feel there are giant gaps in the information you are getting from the standard deck and find yourself wishing for extra.

Do The Cards Include Playing Card Inserts, and Do You Need Them?

Many decks, particularly the more traditional decks, include playing card inserts, as that's how the cards were originally designed back in 1799. Because I began reading Lenormand with a deck that didn't have them at all, I tend not to see them as hugely important to the meanings themselves. It should be noted that they often do not correspond to playing card meanings in traditional cartomancy. So for me, they have never been a necessary or a core part of the Lenormand system, and I have never used the cards this way.

Be aware, however, that many readers feel they get additional nuanced meanings from the playing card references, the court cards, and suits, and feel they deepen the meanings. I don't tend to use them much myself: as you know, I prefer to focus entirely on the core meaning of the card's primary symbol and I think that's where the strength of Lenormand lies. However, if you wish to deepen your Lenormand experience by incorporating the playing card inserts and they do have meaning for you, you will need to pick a deck that does have them.

Do The Cards Contain Other Information e.g. interpretation inserts?

Some decks include interpretative notes, either with basic card meanings or, as in the case of the more traditional decks, descriptive verses. So depending on you & your confidence with the card meanings, you may find these either a help or a hindrance.

I would say if you are forever flicking from list to list, and are not yet confident about card meanings, it might be helpful for you to have them as an *aide-memoire*. I think the descriptive verses are a nice traditional touch, but again, would still prefer to focus for myself on the underlying meanings of the card symbols rather than have them written out for me there.

How Large Are The Cards?

Finally, depending on the layouts you tend to do most often, the size of the cards can be a consideration. I personally prefer to choose decks that are more or less normal playing-card size: some decks, although lovely, are much, much, larger and thus more difficult to handle. If you tend to do Grand Tableaus quite frequently, it is probably better to choose a smaller deck, as otherwise you're going to need a lot of space!

Practice Readings

In this section, I'll give you some examples of various layouts, some general, some with questions, and you can try them out for yourself. Where possible, try to come up with a "story" for the cards in the context given. Then check against my interpretations, which are given at the end of the book.

3-Card Practice Reading 1

Q: This is a blind reading. What do these cards reveal about the past, present and future?

Ring—Fox—Letter

_____

_____

_____

3-Card Practice Reading 2

Q: A friend asks for a reading around a current situation. What story do her cards tell?

Snake— Birds—Heart

_____

_____

_____

3-Card Practice Reading 3

Q: Ben has applied for a job at a particular company. What do the cards tell him about it?

Tree—Clouds—Tower

_____

_____

_____

3-Card Practice Reading 4

Q: Julie is planning to start a new fitness regime. What do the cards tell her about it?

Crossroads—Bear—Tree

_____

_____

_____

5-Card Practice Reading 1

Q: Paula wants a general reading. What's coming up for her this week?

Key—Stars—Tower—Clouds—Clover

_____

_____

_____

_____

_____

_____

5-Card Practice Reading 2

Q: Kelly wants to know what's coming up in her love life. What do the cards indicate?

Stars—Dog—Lily—Mice—Bouquet

_____

_____

_____

_____

_____

_____

5-Card Practice Reading 3

Q: Dan is feeling unsure of his life and work direction. What do the cards say about his situation?

House—Man—Moon—Whip—Fish

_____

_____

_____

_____

_____

_____

5-Card Practice Reading 4

Q: Katie wants to know what actions she should take to ensure success with an upcoming project. What do the cards suggest?

Sun—Garden—Book—Tower—Child

_____

_____

_____

_____

_____

_____

9-Card Practice Reading 1

Q: Jamie has asked what he needs to do to bring more luck into his life.

You choose the Clover as a keycard.

22 CROSSROADS	16 STARS	9 BOUQUET
23 MICE	2 CLOVER	4 HOUSE
28 MAN	33 KEY	20 GARDEN

_____

_____

_____

_____

_____

_____

_____

9-Card Practice Reading 2

Q: Michelle's been through a tough period when she's felt like she's been stuck. She wants to know how she might get past it. You choose the Mountain as the keycard.

24	36	11
HEART	CROSS	WHIP

8	21	17
COFFIN	MOUNTAIN	STORKS

7	26	13
SNAKE	BOOK	CHILD

_____

_____

_____

_____

_____

_____

9-Card Practice Reading 3

Here's an example of a key-card free reading. So although the question contains a potential focus area, we've decided to pull the cards randomly in answer to the question, and just see what they reveal.

Q: Lori wants to know about her financial situation. The cards she pulls in answer to that question are as follows:

30	17	18
LILY	STORKS	DOG

19	20	25
TOWER	GARDEN	RING

12	31	24
BIRDS	SUN	HEART

The Grand Tableau Practice Reading

Q: What's coming up for Miranda in the next six months?

She'd like a general picture but also more detail about her career situation, her home life, things she should watch out for and areas where she is likely to have good luck and positivity.

31 SUN	5 TREE	23 MICE	8 COFFIN	13 CHILD	1 RIDER	33 KEY	24 HEART	18 DOG
22 CROSSROADS	29 WOMAN	17 STORKS	26 BOOK	21 MOUNTAIN	11 WHIP	10 SCYTHE	16 STARS	27 LETTER
12 BIRDS	30 LILY	6 CLOUDS	28 MAN	36 CROSS	3 SHIP	9 BOUQUET	4 HOUSE	32 MOON
14 FOX	19 TOWER	15 BEAR	35 ANCHOR	7 SNAKE	20 GARDEN	34 FISH	25 RING	2 CLOVER

_____

_____

_____

_____

ANSWERS

Exercise II Answers
Test Yourself On Card Meanings

1: Nouns: Things, People, Concepts
Which cards might you associate with the following?

Attractiveness: Bouquet
New Start: Storks
Burdens: Cross
Uncertainty: Clouds
Marriage: Ring
Emotion: Moon
Trouble: Snake
Breakup: Scythe
Papers: Letter
Business: Fish
Ambition: Stars
Family: Home
Friendship: Dog
Officialdom: Tower
Education: Book
Success: Sun
Good Fortune: Clover
Delays: Mountain
Young Person: Child
Social Life: Garden
Conversation: Birds
Stability: Anchor

Conflict: Whip
Travel: Ship
Ending: Coffin
Visitor: Rider

2: Adjectives, Modifiers, Descriptors

Mature: Lily
Verbal: Birds
Anxious: Mice
Written: Letter
Celebrity: Star
Happy: Sun
Public: Garden
Important: Key
Financial: Bear
Corporate: Tower
Negative: Snake
Committed: Ring
Lovely: Bouquet
Harsh: Whip
Karmic: Tree
Fresh: Storks
Healthy: Tree
Secure: Anchor
Masculine: Man
Naive: Child
Moody: Moon

Secret: Book
Domestic: Home
Isolated: Mountain
Arrogant: Tower
Confusing: Clouds
Friendly: Dog

3: Nouns, Things, People II

Which nouns—things, people etc—might you link with the following cards?

Fish: Business, Enterprise, Independence
Whip: Conflict, Argument
Clouds: Confusion, Uncertainty
Crossroads: Options
Storks: New Start
Scythe: Split, Decision
Coffin: Death, Ending
Bouquet: Pleasure, Loveliness, Beauty
Tower: Government, Officialdom, Building
Stars: Celebrity, Ambition
Book: Education, Knowledge
House: Home, Family
Garden: Social Life
Dog: Friend, Friendship, Ally
Ship: Journey

Sun: Success
Tree: Health, Karma
Mountain: Delay, Isolation
Cross: Burden, Depression
Heart: Love, Love Life
Ring: Marriage, Commitment, Deal
Birds: Conversation, Meeting
Lily: Age, Maturity, Older Man
Moon: Emotion, Creativity
Rider: Visitor, New Person
Anchor: Stability
Fox: Work, Career, Deception

4: Adjectives, Modifiers, Descriptors II

Which adjectives might you link with these cards?

Snake: Untrustworthy, Problematic
Lily: Mature, Experienced, Old
Child: Naive, Young, Immature
Scythe: Decisive
Bouquet: Beautiful, Pleasant, Attractive
Tree: Healthy, Karmic
Heart: Romantic, Loving, Passionate
Key: Important
Fox: Deceitful, Cunning, Work-Related
Mice: Worried, Anxious
Book: Educated, Knowledgeable

Cross: Troubled, Guilty
Ship: Travelling, Mobile
Moon: Emotional, Creative, Adored
Fish: Free, Independent, Business-Related
Clover: Lucky
Rider: Upcoming, Approaching, Visiting
Anchor: Stable, Lasting
Tower: Official, Corporate, Arrogant
House: Domestic, Family-Related
Bear: Financial, Powerful, Protective
Ring: Married, Committed
Mountain: Stuck, Blocked, Delayed, Lonely
Garden: Sociable, Public
Birds: Talkative, Communicative
Letter: Written

Exercise IV Answers
Test Yourself On Card Combinations

What could these combinations mean?

Man + Scythe: Decisive man
Fox + Anchor : Stable or permanent job
Ring + Sun: Successful marriage or deal
Woman + Bouquet: Pretty woman
Snake + Scythe: Accident, Harm, Hurt
Bear + Clover: Win, Financial good fortune

Tree + Cross: Depression, Health issue
Book + Key: Significant knowledge, Discovery
Key + Woman: Female soulmate
Stars + Ship: Rocket; progress towards goals

Which pairs of cards could represent these?

A Marriage Ending: Ring + Scythe
Lovely options: Crossroads + Bouquet
Health worries: Mice + Tree
Friendly advice: Birds + Dog
A difficult job: Fox + Whip
Secret affair: Heart + Book
Celebrity artist: Moon + Stars, Stars + Moon
Therapy: Tree + Dog, Dog + Cross
Financial luck: Clover + Bear
Business meeting: Birds + Fish
Sexy woman: Woman + Whip
Travel delays: Mountain + Ship
Arrogant man: Man + Tower
Great happiness: Clover + Sun, Sun + Clover, Sun + Stars

Exercise VI Answers
Telling Stories With Lenormand

Question (General): What Is Coming Up This Week?

	Stork	Whip	Bear
Meaning:	**Change**	**Discipline/Conflict**	**Money/Power**

Cards 1+ 3 Combined around Card 2

Changes + Money/Power around Conflict

Meaning: **Money or power changes due to an argument or discipline**

Cards 1+ 2 Combined **Change + Discipline**

Meaning: **Forced or driven changes**

Cards 2+ 3 Combined **Discipline + Power**

Meaning: **Powerful or forceful discipline or drive**

Cards 1+2, 2+3 **Forced or driven changes; powerful drive**

Q: What is coming up this week? (General)

A: Changes are brought about due to power or force; forced changes come about

Question (Career): John wants a raise at work. What would you advise him?

	Stork	**Whip**	**Bear**
Meaning (Career)	**Change**	**Conflict/Discipline**	**Money/Power**

Cards 1+ 3 Combined around Card 2

Change + Money/Power around Discipline/Conflict

Meaning: **Money or power changes happen around conflict or push**

Cards 1+ 2 Combined **Change + Conflict/Discipline**

Meaning: **Pushed or argued-for changes**

Cards 2+ 3 Combined **Conflict/Discipline + Money or Power**

Meaning: **Money or power dispute or push**

Cards 1+2, 2+3 **Argued/Pushed for Change, Money/Power Dispute or Drive**

Q: John wants a raise at work. What would you advise him?

A: It isn't going to just be handed to him on a plate. He is going to need to push and argue for changes to be made to his salary, possibly with the powers-that-be.

Question (Relationships): Your daughter's upset about her relationship. What's been going on?

	Stork	Whip	Bear
Meaning (Relationship)	**Change**	**Arguments**	**Power**

Cards 1+ 3 Combined around Card 2 : **Change + Power around Arguments**

Meaning: **Forceful or forced changed in arguments**

Cards 1+ 2 Combined **Change + Arguments**

Meaning: **Arguments have changed**

Cards 2+ 3 Combined **Arguments + Power/force**

Meaning: **Powerful or forceful arguments**

Cards 1+2, 2+3 **There's been a change in argument style. They have become more forceful**

Q: Your daughter's upset about her relationship. What's been going on?

A: _ This seems like things could be getting kind of abusive. There's been a change in argument style and they are becoming more forceful or physical.

Answers to Practice Readings

Obviously, the exact ways we choose to tell the "story" of a reading may differ from person to person, but hopefully, if you've considered both the contexts and the questions for each practice layout, we should have come up with broadly similar interpretations.

3-Card Practice Reading 1

Q: This is a blind reading. What do these cards reveal about the past, present and future?

*A: In the past, we see an agreement, promise or commitment (**Ring**). Perhaps a contract of some sort. The present situation is about work, day to day survival; what the querent is doing to put food on the table (**Fox**). Coming up ahead will be either some news, a message, or a written document of some kind (**Letter**) connected with this.*

3-Card Practice Reading 2

Q: A friend asks for a reading around a current situation. What story do her cards tell?

*A: The cards show a betrayal or problem of some sort (**Snake**), a conversation or communication (**Birds**) connected with her love life (**Heart**). With the Birds in the centre, the reading is primarily about this conversation, during which she is let down (**Snake-Heart**). She is let down verbally (**Snake-Birds**) and it is a romantic or love-related conversation (**Birds-Heart**). The reading doesn't tell us whether this has already happened or is still to come; either way, it looks as if there is a degree of heartbreak in the air.*

3-Card Practice Reading 3

Q: Ben has applied for a job at a particular company. What do the cards tell him about it?

*A: The cards in this context show health, vitality and growth (**Tree**), a lack of clarity or something murky (**Clouds**) and an established organisation (**Tower**). With the Clouds as the* *middle card, this lack of clarity is central to the reading, and it seems to be about the health of this company (**Tree-Tower**). It's likely that company health or growth is in some doubt (**Tree-Clouds**) and that the company may be purposely obscuring or hiding the reality of this (**Clouds-Tower**). If I were Ben, I would be trying to find out more about the future stability of this company for my own security before making any decisions around this role.*

3-Card Practice Reading 4

Q: Julie is planning to start a new fitness regime. What do the cards tell her about it?

*A: The cards in this context show options or choices (**Crossroads**), physical strength & diet (**Bear**) and health and vitality (**Tree**). Physical strength & diet is at the heart of the reading (Bear), which is all about making healthy choices (**Crossroads-Tree**). It looks as if she has a range of strength-building options (**Crossroads-Bear**) that will take Julie to a healthy physique (**Bear-Tree**). Because of the focus on the Bear rather than, say, the Whip or Heart, (which would represent sport or cardio) the cards seem to be suggesting that weight-training and strength-building is more the way Julie should go with the regime she chooses.*

5-Card Practice Reading 1

Q: Paula wants a general reading. What's coming up for her this week?

*A: The cards individually show something fated or of significance (**Key**), Paula's hopes or ambitions (**Stars**), either status, a company or officialdom of some kind (**Tower**), uncertainty and doubt (**Clouds**) and luck and good fortune (**Clover**). The Tower at the centre of the reading means that this sense of officialdom or status is at the heart of what is coming up. Paula may have corporate ambitions or a desire to be established or have status in some way (**Stars-Tower**) although there is something uncertain or vague about this (**Tower-Clouds**). Perhaps she feels she doesn't deserve it? Overall, it looks as though something of great significance will happen to her this week by chance (**Key-Clover**), a twist of fate connected with ambitions and hopes that are perhaps loose or dreamt of rather than something Paula consciously focuses on (**Stars-Clouds**).*

Reading the cards in a chain shows us that these hopes and dreams are important or fated (*Key-Stars*), involve high-status ambitions and thinking big (*Stars-Tower*), and although she is perhaps uncertain or unclear about the status aspect (*Tower-Clouds*), not being too certain may actually be what will bring her good fortune this week. (*Clouds-Clover*)

5-Card Practice Reading 2

Q: Kelly wants to know what's coming up in her love life. What do the cards indicate?

*A: The cards individually in this context show Kelly's hopes and dreams (**Stars**), a friendship or companion (**Dog**), age, wisdom or an older person, possibly an older male (**Lily**), anxiety and nerves (**Mice**) and something lovely, a blessing of some kind or even a wedding (**Bouquet**). The Lily at the centre of the reading shows that age or wisdom (or an older person) is at the heart of what's ahead. The cards indicate that this may be an old or older friend (**Dog-Lily**) and there is some kind of anxiety about age or growing older (**Lily-Mice**). It looks as though those hopes and dreams will be achieved (**Stars-Bouquet**) but that there is some anxiety involved around the friend or friendship (**Lily-Mice**). Reading the cards in a chain, we see the hopes and dreams associated with a friend (**Stars-Dog**), an old friendship or older male friend), this person's nerves or some worry about the age factor (**Lily-Mice**) but which are not serious - a case of the butterflies if anything or anticipation and are positive in outcome (**Mice-Bouquet**).*

5-Card Practice Reading 3

Q: Dan is feeling unsure of his life and work direction. What do the cards say about his situation?

*A: The cards individually in this context represent Dan's home or family (**House**), Dan himself (**Man**), creativity or feelings (**Moon**), hard work, conflict or competition (**Whip**) and business (**Fish**.) As the querent card appears in the reading, we can use it as the keycard rather than the central card, the moon. What we see is that it's about Dan's home or family life (**House-Man**) and that he is a sensitive, artistic or creative man (**Man-Moon**). Mirroring the cards around him indicates a creative or emotional home or family (**House-Moon**). If we mirror the other cards as* usual, we get perhaps a business domain or name (**House-Fish**) and Dan as also probably quite hardworking, competitive man (**Man-Fish**). Reading the cards in a chain, we have Dan's home or family (**House-Man**), himself as an emotional or creative man (**Man-Moon**), difficult or harsh or conflicting feelings (**Moon-Whip**) and business competition, conflict or hard work (**Whip-Fish**). The cards here don't seem to give any advice really, but perhaps reflect why he is feeling unsure and conflicted. Is he doing what really feels like 'home' to him? Or are his feelings about what business 'should' look like getting in the way? With a reading like this, it would perhaps be useful to do a further 9-card spread around the Whip to dig a little deeper into what the conflict issue is about.

5-Card Practice Reading 4

Q: Katie wants to know what actions she should take to ensure success with an upcoming project. What do the cards suggest?

*A: First of all, we don't have any information about the type of project itself here. It could of course be a book, given that the Book is at the heart of the reading. Individually, the cards show success and positivity (**Sun**), a group, public or sharing (**Garden**), a book, knowledge or learning (**Book**), something official or established (**Tower**) and probably, in this context, someone in the early stages of something (**Child**). At the centre of the reading we have a suggestion of either the book (if it is a book) or knowledge shared publicly, perhaps in a group (**Garden-Book**), and what looks like established knowledge or learning, perhaps an education setting or college (**Book-Tower**), and around this, the cards show a beginner or student's positive and success (**Sun-Child**) as well as some sort of established or official group (**Garden-Tower**). The cards seem to be strongly hinting that Katie would do well by taking a course of study where she can share knowledge with others, perhaps in a class. Looking at the cards in a chain we see a public or group success (**Sun-Garden**) in perhaps a class (**Garden-Book**) at a college or learning organisation (**Book-Tower**) for those who are beginners (**Tower-Child**). So the actions the cards suggest Katie takes for success in this project is for her to take a class or course of learning where she can share knowledge with others.*

9-Card Practice Reading 1

Q: Jamie has asked what he needs to do to bring more luck into his life. You choose the Clover as a keycard.

*A: First, we look at the diamond around the keycard to determine the overall picture. Jamie's desires seem quite anxiety-driven (**Stars-Mice**), the worries are significant (**Mice-Key**), it's connected with the importance of a house, home life or even his name (**Key-House**) and possibly his desire for his dream house or for his name to be well-known, celebrity, even (**House-Stars**). The luck Jamie's thinking of means taking ambitious paths (**Crossroads-Stars**) and possibly going for prizes or awards (**Stars-Bouquet**). The answer in the centre row appears to show him worrying about luck (**Mice-Clover**) and the good fortune of his name - his reputation in other words (**Clover-House.**). Additionally, we see Jamie himself (**Man**) as a person of some public importance, out in the world (**Man-Key-Garden**). It appears he's coming to this issue from a place where he's had many worries and anxiety about a number of things (**Crossroads-Mice-Man**). The cards strongly indicate Jamie has big ambitions and there are significant opportunities and life-changing opportunities around at the moment (**Stars-Clover-Key**). Ahead, are the public blessings he is looking for, perhaps a happy family event, or something that really puts his name on the map (**Bouquet-House-Garden**).*

9-Card Practice Reading 2

Q: Michelle's been through a tough period when she's felt like she's been stuck. She wants to know how she might get past it. You choose the Mountain as the keycard.

*A: As you will see, because of the keycard, the reading ends up focusing more on the problem and its causes itself than on solutions, although it does give us quite a bit of information. Looking first at the issues around this stuck period, we see that Michelle has felt pressured or burdened in some way by something finishing (**Cross-Coffin**), perhaps a period of education or learning ending or some knowledge that brought an ending about (**Coffin-Book**). We can also see, though, that* *around this new start and new knowledge or learning coming (Book-Storks) although this may also be associated with new pressures (**Storks-Cross**). Sitting above this blockage, the cards indicate a troubled time: a heavy heart, in some way, perhaps a draining love relationship (**Heart-Cross**) and some serious pressure or even abuse or self-flagellation or guilt (**Cross-Whip**) It looks as if Michelle has been giving herself a really hard time. The middle row shows us that there's a possibility of a fresh start after this particular blockage has ended (**Coffin-Mountain-Storks**), and the bottom row tells us that perhaps the situation involved an unpleasant secret or discovery (**Snake-Book**), possibly involving a child (**Book-Child**). Certainly, the first column shows the situation has a background of the end of what is likely a love relationship (**Heart-Coffin**) in the circumstances of a betrayal (**Coffin-Snake**). The final nail, perhaps. The present shows some knowledge or learning weighing extremely heavy on her and causing this blockage or stuck feeling (**Cross-Mountain-Book**). Michelle needs to move on but it looks as though it will still require some effort to be made to get over this into new beginnings (**Whip-Storks**) and a fresh new start (**Storks-Child**). Moving from the past into the future and a blocked heart (**Heart-Mountain**) will involve perhaps starting right from the beginning again (**Mountain-Child**) and again, that it's going to take a concerted effort to get over the betrayal involved (**Snake-Mountain-Whip**). This is a great example of where it is sometimes better not to choose a keycard, and to leave the cards to fall where they will. In this case, I would probably do another, key-card free reading, in order to answer Michelle's question more accurately.*

9-Card Practice Reading 3

Q: Lori wants to know about her financial situation.

*A: The first observation here is that although the question Lori asked was about money, there was no **Bear** card appearing in the reading. That's not a problem in itself but just to be aware that the circumstances surrounding Lori's question about money may have other issues or circumstances at core.*

Instead, at the centre of the reading, is the Garden card. This represents Lori's social world, her public life - and possibly, given the context of the reading, the marketplace. Around this issue, the

*Storks-Tower-Sun-Ring diamond gives us an overall picture that involves a kind of official or corporate or established new beginning; a successful establishment or structure; relationship, agreement or contract success; a brand new agreement or deal. So it sounds as if Lori's financial fate might revolve around a business situation of some sort and public perception of it. Looking at the top row of cards representing what's governing this core issue of the marketplace, the Lily-Storks-Dog cards show a fresh maturity, new wisdom; friendly new start, possibly the return of an old friend from the past. The middle row, at the heart of the reading, shows some sort of public or market organisation (**Tower-Garden**) and some sort of agreement with it; a membership perhaps (**Garden-Ring**)? It also indicates a successful and positive conversation about something something Lori truly loves (**Birds-Sun-Heart**). Appearing in the past or background of the situation is what looks like some sort of media organisation experience (**Lily-Tower** = organisational or official experience, Tower-Birds = communication organisation) which I think is now giving Lori a positive and successful head start in the marketplace (**Storks-Garden-Sun**). To me, it strongly sounds as if she is a marketeer of some kind or a public relations person. Ahead, we see what would usually look like a loving marriage to a friend or companion, but in this context could mean an agreement, partnership with or even a donation from a caring supporter, fan or friend (**Dog-Ring-Heart**). Looking at influences from past to future in the diagonals, indicate Lori's past public experience of sharing the love (**Lily-Garden-Heart**) and communicating with her supporters and public (Birds-**Garden**-Dog) will be important to her financial situation as a whole.*

The Grand Tableau Practice Reading

Q: What's coming up for Miranda in the next six months?
She'd like a general picture but also more detail about her career situation, her home life, things she should watch out for and areas where she is likely to have success.

The first thing to look at is the first four cards and then the corners for an overall picture of the next six months. So from this we get that this period for Miranda will represent a healthy and *growing success (**Sun-Tree**) with perhaps some anxiety about it but those worries coming to an end (**Mice-Coffin**). The corner cards show very fortunate success (**Sun-Clover**) and friendly or supportive work, perhaps an advisor (**Fox-Dog**).*

*Looking for Miranda's card, we see her card (**Woman**) appears in the house of the **Whip** (position 11) so it is a period of hard work and effort for her. She is also impacted by what is going on at home (the House reflecting her), something to do with writing, perhaps journalism or documenting and a sense of maturation or even an older man (the **Letter** and **Lily** mirroring her). She is being knighted by money and work (**Fox and Bear**), but also an ending connected with a male (**Coffin and Man.**). Her position in the spread shows she has a lot coming up but that she also relatively in control of things.*

*Reading the cards around her as a 9-card spread, we see the growth of options or pathways, a maturing of her options and a new, more mature beginning that indicates growth and development (**Tree-Crossroads-Lily-Storks**). On her mind is her burgeoning success but also a degree of anxiety about it. (**Sun-Tree-Mice**) and this period will involve a new start, new Miranda, with new options (**Crossroads-Woman-Storks**). At the same time, there'll be a lack of clarity or confusion about old or past communications, or with an older man (**Birds-Lily-Clouds**). In the recent past, she seems to have communicated a number of successes (**Sun-Crossroads-Birds**) and is now in a position of mature or experienced growth (**Tree-Woman-Lily**). Immediately ahead is a new start of some kind, although she seems to be experiencing some anxiety about this as well as lack of clarity about what it actually will be. (**Mice-Storks-Clouds**).*

*Her development and growth is a key issue for her (**Tree**) and the maturation into a more established or better status position (**Lily-Tower**). Miranda has made multiple choices (**Crossroads**). Ahead of her is the start of a new period of learning or knowledge (Storks-Book) although it doesn't look like it will come easy: things may be subject to delays (**Book-Mountain**) and tough obstacles to get over (**Mountain-Whip**), which may appear quite suddenly (**Whip-*

Scythe). This is followed by what is most likely some kind of written decision (**Scythe-Letter**). It all seems worth it in the end though: the cards indicate hopeful news or a positive result, with goals achieved (**Letter-Stars**).

At this point, we can choose how much more detail we wish to go into. Here, you could just read all the horizontals and verticals and that would give you a great deal of general information. However, Miranda specifically asked about her career situation, her home life, things she should watch out for and areas where she is likely to have success. So to get a closer look at these, I would focus on the **Fox** (or **Fish**), the House, the Snake, and the Sun.

Miranda's Career: The Fox card here is appearing in the House of the **Man** *(28)*, which is interesting given the earlier part of the reading, & indicates that it's very connected with a man. Her work life is being reflected by the **Dog** card, indicating friendship, support and advice, and is being mirrored by both success (**Sun**), and good fortune & opportunities (**Clover**). Her work life is being knighted by Miranda herself (**Woman**) and the **Clouds** card, showing there's a sense of uncertainty, lack of direction or vagueness within her. Because of the card's position, there aren't many cards around it, but what it does show is conversation or communication, probably with someone older (**Birds-Lily**) and in an official capacity (**Tower**).

Miranda's Home Life: The **House** card here (which can represent family as well her own home) is appearing in the House of the **Book** *(26)*: in other words, learning, knowledge and discoveries. It is being reflected by Miranda herself (**Woman**), and mirrored by some news (**Letter**) as well as someone older, again, perhaps an older man (**Lily**) or just maturity in general. Miranda's home-life is being knighted by some sort of public difficulty or having a hard time out in the world (**Whip-Garden**) as well as an indication that true friendship will prove important (**Key-Dog**). Looking around the card, we see that the hopeful news and written decision (**Scythe-Letter-Stars**) appears to be about her home life, that her home life will bring her emotional or creative happiness (**Bouquet-House-Moon**) and there are signs of a fortunate agreement of some kind connected perhaps with business or freedom (**Fish-Ring-Clover**). A positive business or *independence decision (**Scythe-Bouquet-Fish**) leads to some kind of home-related agreement and documentation (**Letter-House-Ring**) which brings extremely lucky and positive feelings and emotions around Miranda's hopes and dreams (**Stars-Moon-Clover**). Definite good vibes here. Decisions around her home-life prove lucky (**Scythe-House-Clover**) and are related to her freedom, perhaps for a home-based business, and her hopes and dreams (**Fish-House-Stars**.)*

*Things Miranda Should Watch Out For: The **Snake** card is falling in the House of the **Moon** (32), so the biggest issues are probably going to be coming from Miranda herself in terms of negative feelings and emotions. The only card reflecting and mirroring this is the **Child** which indicates either immaturity or naivety. In terms of the cards that are knighting the Snake, we have the **Clouds**, so that sense of uncertainty will play a part, the struggle with learning she has and how this training period won't be easy (**Book-Whip**) although ultimately, it should be seen positively because it results in good (**Bouquet**).*

*Miranda's areas of Success: The **Sun** card appears in the House of the **Rider** (1) which shows success on its way. The fact it's also reflected by the **Clover** card is very good news indeed, and its being mirrored by the **Dog** and **Fox** cards shows a lot of it will be to do with her friendships and support and career. Miranda's success card is being knighted by the **Lily** and the **Storks**, so a new beginning is well-starred and connected either with her own maturity or an older person. Again, the cards' position doesn't show a lot around it but what is there is positive: a sense of flourishing and growth (**Tree**), choices (**Crossroad**) and Miranda herself (**Woman**).*

FINALLY!

Thank you so much for reading this guide. I hope you've found the information about working with Lenormand and practice exercises and readings helpful, and now feel fully equipped more able to apply it to your own readings.

Do join me on the Lozzy's Lenormand website **www.lozzyslenormand.com**, where you'll find further guidance and tips on card layouts and readings, Lenormand decks, readings, predictions, freebies and much, much more!

Look forward to seeing you there!

All best, and happy Lenormand-reading!

Lozzy Phillips

About The Author

Lozzy Phillips is a freelance writer and card-reader from the UK, who spent many years working in both teaching and publishing before embarking on a freelance existence. She has lived and travelled all over the world—notably South America, and both Central and Western Europe — but is now settled back in her home country, and lives in Kent. She loves reading, cooking, writing fiction, current affairs—and earth-witchery in all its forms.

Made in the USA
Las Vegas, NV
13 October 2021